ADVANCED LEVEL

Skimming & Scanning

SECOND EDITION

D1303286

EDWARD B. FRY, Ph.D.
Professor Emeritus
Rutgers University

JAMESTOWN PUBLISHERS
a division of NTC/CONTEMPORARY PUBLISHING GROUP
Lincolnwood, Illinois USA

Skimming and Scanning
Advanced Level
Second Edition

Cover and text design: Deborah Hulsey Christie

ISBN: 0-89061-674-4

Published by Jamestown Publishers,
a division of NTC/Contemporary Publishing Group, Inc.,
4255 West Touhy Avenue,
Lincolnwood (Chicago), Illinois 60646-1975 U.S.A.

8 9 0 GW 11 10 9 8 7 6 5 4

Foreword

Skimming and Scanning, Advanced Level is designed for students in high school and college.

This Second Edition of *Skimming & Scanning* contains updated and more current scanning drills as well as design and presentation improvements.

Some people use the terms *skimming* and *scanning* interchangeably. However, in this book we will use them to indicate two different types of reading activities.

Skimming means the very rapid reading of a whole article to get the main ideas and some of the supporting details—but not all of the details. Skimming implies an intentionally lowered comprehension so that maximum speed can be obtained.

Scanning, on the other hand, is a locational skill. The reader already knows what to look for; the job is simply to locate the information. For example, when using the telephone directory, you already know the person's name. You simply scan down the column until you find it, and then read the number opposite the name. You certainly do not "read" the whole column of names. Scanning is also done in a wide range of other situations, such as looking up the time a train departs or the time a TV program will be on the air. This book contains a variety of scanning exercises which are interesting to students and very practical. The student should strive for *efficiency;* this requires *speed* plus *accuracy.*

Skimming and scanning are valuable reading skills which will make you a more efficient and flexible reader. The information and exercises provided in this text were designed to help you master these important reading techniques. Careful study now will prepare you for proficient reading of a wide variety of material and for a lifetime of reading enjoyment.

Edward Fry

Acknowledgments

Skimming section adapted from *Teaching Faster Reading* by Edward B. Fry. Copyright © 1963 by Cambridge University Press and reprinted with their permission.

"Alexander Dolgun's Story: An American in the Gulag." From *Alexander Dolgun's Story: An American in the Gulag* by Alexander Dolgun. Copyright © 1975 by Alexander Dolgun. Reprinted by permission of Alfred A. Knopf, Inc.

"To Sir, with Love." From *To Sir, with Love* by E. R. Braithwaite. Copyright © 1959 by E. R. Braithwaite. Reprinted by permission of Prentice-Hall, Inc.

"Alive: The Story of the Andes Survivors." From *Alive: The Story of the Andes Survivors* by Piers Paul Read. Copyright © 1974 by Piers Paul Read. Reprinted by permission of J. B. Lippincott Company.

"Roots." From *Roots* by Alex Haley. Copyright © 1976 by Alex Haley. Reprinted by permission of Doubleday & Company, Inc.

"Reincarnation and 13 Pairs of Socks" by Jerry Kirshenbaum. Reprinted from *Sports Illustrated*, March 28, 1977. Copyright © 1977 by Time, Inc. and reprinted with their permission.

"Sharks: The Silent Savages." From *Sharks: The Silent Savages* by Theo W. Brown. Copyright © 1973 by Theo W. Brown. Reprinted by permission of Little, Brown and Co. and that of Angus and Robertson Publishers, Sydney.

"My Early Life." From *My Early Life, A Roving Commission* by Winston Churchill. Copyright © 1930 by Charles Scribner's Sons and reprinted with their permission.

"Hour of Gold, Hour of Lead." From *Hour of Gold, Hour of Lead* by Anne Morrow Lindbergh. Copyright © 1973 by Anne Morrow Lindbergh. Reprinted by permission of Harcourt Brace Jovanovich, Inc.

"Centennial." From *Centennial* by James A. Michener. Copyright © 1974 by Marjay Productions, Inc. Reprinted by permission of Random House, Inc.

"Body Language." From *Body Language* by Julius Fast. Copyright © 1970 by Julius Fast. Reprinted by permission of M. Evans and Company, Inc.

Telephone directory page reprinted by permission of New England Telephone and Telegraph Company.

"Best Sellers" reprinted from *Los Angeles Times*, November 13, 1988. Copyright © 1988 by The Los Angeles Times Company and reprinted with their permission.

Billboard "Hot 100," *Billboard* "Hot Black," *Billboard* "Hot Latin," and *Billboard* "Hot Country" reprinted from *Billboard*, November 1, 1988. Copyright © 1988 by Billboard Publications, Inc. and reprinted with their permission.

"The Wolf Gets a Better Image with Biologist's Help" by Boyce Rensberger. Reprinted from the *New York Times*, February 16, 1977. Copyright © 1977 by The New York Times Company and reprinted with their permission.

Reprinted with permission from TV GUIDE® Magazine. Copyright © 1988 by Triangle Publications, Inc., Radnor, Pennsylvania.

Contents

Part 1: Skimming

Part 2: Scanning

Scanning Drills (continued)

Answer Keys

Graphs

Picture Credits

Part 1: Skimming

How to Skim

One sign of a good reader is flexibility. Good readers are able to adapt their reading skills to meet the demands of the material they wish to cover. When reading easier textbooks, novels, and newspapers, for example, good readers use an average rate of speed. This speed might vary from 250 to 500 words per minute with about 70 percent comprehension.

However, there is a great deal of material which readers would like to cover either because they are interested in a particular field or simply because they wish to be well informed. Using an average rate of speed to cover this large amount of reading matter would take more time than is usually available. In addition, there is often no need to read such material with a high degree of comprehension. For this type of reading matter, flexible readers are able to adapt their reading speed to suit their purposes. When good readers wish to cover large amounts of material quickly, they skim.

What Skimming Is

Skimming is reading at the fastest possible speed. It is used when a reader wishes to cover material in a hurry. It is also used when high comprehension is not required. This does not mean that in skimming you should accept a ridiculously low standard of comprehension; it merely means that in some instances it may be appropriate to accept a level of comprehension somewhat lower than that obtained at average reading speeds.

Skimming vs. Average Reading. In order to achieve a high rate of skimming, it is important to note some basic differencess between skimming and average reading. In average reading you do not skip any material; you cover the entire amount of reading matter. This does not mean that your eyes fixate, or stop, on every word, but neither does it mean that you can skip any whole sentences or parts of paragraphs. In skimming, however, it is fair to leave out material. In many cases you may leave out half or three-quarters of a paragraph if you feel you've grasped the main idea. Thus skimming differs from average reading in the fact that chunks of material may be selectively left out.

Comprehension. Skimming also differs from average reading in that a lowered level of comprehension becomes acceptable. In average reading, you attempt to achieve as much comprehension as you can. This usually means 70 or 80 percent, as you are probably not willing to pay the price of slowness in order to get a higher comprehension score. However, in average reading, you would aim toward achieving as high a comprehension score as you could manage while maintaining an average reading speed. In skimming, one intentionally accepts less comprehension. This means that 50 percent would be a good average skimming comprehension while 60 percent would be a little better than average.

If during skimming you consistently score 70 or 80 percent, it means that you are not skimming nearly fast enough and should speed up, no matter how fast you were skimming when you scored 70 percent. Conversely, a persistent score of 30 or 40 percent is too low. Occasionally you may hit 40 percent on a skimming exercise, but if you consistently do this it means that you are not skimming correctly or are going too fast for your ability.

Speed. It is difficult to say exactly how fast skimming should be, but a safe rule of thumb is that it should be twice as fast as your average reading speed. If, for example, your average reading speed is 400 words per minute, you could achieve a skimming rate of 800 words per minute or better.

Thus we see emerging some of the characteristics of skimming, such as (1) a selective leaving out of parts of the material, (2) an intentional acceptance of a lowered degree of comprehension, and (3) an extremely rapid rate.

The following table shows various reading rates of the good reader. Notice that flexible readers have three reading speeds: slow, average, and fast. Each of these speeds is appropriate for a specific type of reading material.

Kind of Reading	Rate	Comprehension
Slow: *Study reading* speed is used when material is difficult or when high comprehension is desired.	200 to 300 wpm	80–90%
Average: An *average reading* speed is used for everyday reading of magazines, newspapers, and easier textbooks.	250 to 500 wpm	70%
Fast: *Skimming* is used when the highest rate is desired. Comprehension is intentionally lower.	800+ wpm	50%

Note also that as reading speed increases, comprehension decreases. When skimming at 800 words per minute, you cannot expect to achieve greater than 50 percent comprehension. Thus, when choosing a reading speed, you must make certain that the comprehension level of the speed you choose is appropriate for the material you wish to read.

Steps for Skimming

Now we come to the problem faced by the student who is about to do a skimming exercise. Precisely what does the student do to achieve an extremely fast rate? What material should be left out?

What to Read. Let us say that you wish to skim a factual article of several thousand words. You should first read the opening paragraph or two at your fastest average rate. That means that you leave out nothing, but go at your top reading speed of 300 or 400 words per minute. Read all of the first several paragraphs in order to get started and to grasp the idea of the story, the setting, a little of the author's style, the tone or mood, and so on. Frequently an author will give an introduction in the first few paragraphs; this will help to give you an overall picture of the story.

What to Leave Out. Once you have a general overview of the story, you must begin to leave out material right away if you are to achieve a skimming rate of 800 words per minute or better. Hence, on the third or fourth paragraph you read only the key sentence, struggle to get the main idea of the paragraph, and skip the second half. Perhaps you will read the key sentences and let your eyes jump down through the paragraph picking up one or two important words, phrases, or numbers.

Finding the Main Idea. In skimming, you should attempt to get the main idea of every paragraph plus a few facts. You cannot hope to pick up all the facts in the story, but you might pick up some facts, names, or numbers.

Sometimes the key sentence will not be the first sentence in the paragraph. In some paragraphs the main idea is located in the middle or at the end. You will then have to spend some time looking for the key sentence.

In addition, you may come to a paragraph which does not have a key sentence at all; that is, the main idea is not summarized in any one sentence. You will then have to hunt around a little in order to find several phrases or sentences which give the main idea. You may even have to read the entire paragraph in order to get its meaning. But having read a paragraph all the way through, you must then skim even faster on the next few paragraphs to make up for lost time.

On the next page, you can see how you might skim an article. Notice that you read all of the first and second paragraphs to get an overview. By the third or fourth paragraph you must begin to leave out material; read only key sentences and phrases to get the main ideas and a few of the details. Note also that, since final paragraphs often summarize, it may be worthwhile to read them more fully.

Skimming must be done "against the clock." That is, you must try to go as fast as you possibly can while leaving out large chunks of material. Be careful to avoid getting interested in the story since this might slow you down and cause you to read unnecessary detail. Skimming is work. It is done when you do not have much time and when you wish to cover material at the fastest possible rate.

Developing Skimming Ability
Set a Goal. When readers first try to skim, they often achieve speeds little better than their average reading rate. But skimming exercises must

HOW TO SKIM

Usually the first paragraph will be read at average speed all the way through. It often contains an introduction or overview of what will be talked about.

Sometimes, however, the second paragraph contains the introduction or overview. In the first paragraph the author might just be "warming up" or saying something clever to attract attention.

Reading a third paragraph completely might be unnecessary but ... ... the main idea is usually contained in the opening sentence ... ... topic sentence ... ...

Besides the first sentence the reader should get some but not all the detail from the rest of the paragraph ... ... names ... ... dates ... ... This tells you nothing ... ...

... ... hence sometimes the main idea is in the middle or at the end of the paragraph.

Some paragraphs merely repeat ideas ... ... Occasionally the main idea can't be found in the opening sentence. The whole paragraph must then be read.

Then leave out a lot of the next paragraph ... ... to make up time ... ...

Remember to keep up a very fast rate ... ... 800 wpm ... ...

Don't be afraid to leave out half or more of each paragraph ... ...

Don't get interested and start to read everything ... ... skimming is work ... ...

... ... Lowered comprehension is expected ... ... 50% ... ... not too low ... ... Skimming practice makes it easier ... ... gain confidence ... ...

... ... Perhaps you won't get anything at all from a few paragraphs ... ... don't worry ... ...

Skimming has many uses ... ... reports ... ... newspapers ... ... supplementary ... ... text ... ...

The ending paragraphs might be read more fully as often they contain a summary.

Remember that the importance of skimming is to get only the author's main ideas at a very fast speed.

be repeated until some established goal, such as 800 words per minute, is reached. You should set a goal that is roughly two times faster than your best average reading rate. (If the class averages 400 words per minute, a general goal of 800 words per minute might be set.)

Re-skim. Those who have difficulty in learning to skim can often be helped by a simple type of exercise which involves skimming the same article several times in succession. For example, if you try to skim an article and get a rate of only 400 words per minute, you should skim the same article again and attempt to get up to 800 words per minute. Perhaps on your second attempt you will get to 600 words per minute. But, on your next time through, you must leave out even more material and go faster until you can achieve a goal of 800 words per minute—even if it is on the third or fourth attempt. Your results might look like this:

	1st Reading	2nd Reading	3rd Reading
Article 1	310 wpm	490 wpm	715 wpm
Article 2	450 wpm	630 wpm	825 wpm
Article 3	675 wpm	910 wpm	
Article 4	850 wpm		

Note the improvement on each successive drill. When using this method of improving your skimming rate, take the comprehension test only after the first time through.

Practice. It is best that your first skimming be done in class. The guidance and supervision of your teacher will get you off to a good start. After that, however, it is good to do some skimming as homework. The more you practice, the better your chance of developing your skills at skimming. Magazine articles and chapters from supplementary textbooks are a good source of material for additional skimming practice.

When practicing your skimming technique outside of class, you should set a goal of 800 words per minute even if repeated practice on the same article is necessary. Check a page or two of the book or magazine to discover the approximate number of words per page. Determine the number of pages you must cover each minute to achieve 800 words.

Check Comprehension. Skimming drills should, of course, be followed by comprehension tests; there is no point in reading material at any rate, including the faster skimming rates, if there is no comprehension. If you are practicing skimming on magazine articles, textbook chapters, or novels for which there are no regular comprehension tests, your teacher may help you check your comprehension by (1) making up a few simple questions, (2) asking you to write a paragraph giving the main points, or (3) having oral questions or class discussion on the passage skimmed.

Another interesting exercise your teacher may ask you to do is skim an article and then write a paragraph stating the main ideas plus a few of the details. You then reread the article at an average reading rate (not leaving out anything but not going at a study rate). After the second reading, you write a second paragraph stating whether or not you felt that your first paragraph was essentially correct, giving the main ideas correctly if they were wrong before, and in either case adding a few more details. Your reading time should be taken, and a words-per-minute score worked out, for each reading.

Skim Regularly. The more often you skim, the more you gain in confidence and the better your chances of making skimming a permanent reading skill. In order to establish skimming as a habit, you should make the skimming of entire magazines or of certain chapters of supplementary textbooks part of your regular reading routine. Use skimming for everyday purposes as often as you can. Once you have become accustomed to skimming and have established the habit, it will prove valuable throughout your life.

Advantages of Skimming

Improves Other Reading Rates. The usefulness of learning how to skim can be seen in many situations. It has been found, for example, that training in skimming has a good effect on other reading speeds. The table on page 10 describes three types of reading—study reading, average reading, and skimming—and shows the corresponding reading rates of a good reader. Learning to skim rapidly can help you improve your speed for study reading and average reading as well.

Keeps You Informed. In addition, there are many times when you can use skimming to get information from material you otherwise would not read. People often have a desire to be generally informed in such fields as political affairs or cultural development and yet don't have the time to read much on these subjects. Skimming will help you keep informed without taking the time that average reading would.

Speeds Supplementary Assignments. As a student, there are times when you will be asked to do supplementary reading for a course. Sometimes the teacher will assign more supplementary reading than you can really cover at an average or study rate. If you skim the supplementary material (not your basic textbooks), you may be pleased and surprised to learn how much of the material you can comprehend at fast skimming rates.

Increases Your Sources of Reference. Skimming is also quite useful in building up a fund of reference information. If, for example, you are instructed to read regularly several journals or reports in a given field, the chances are that not all the articles in the journal or report will be of equal importance. It is often satisfactory if you know merely of the existence of the article and perhaps its main idea. At a later time, you may be able to cite the main idea of the article in class, seeming quite well informed. This is not dishonest. You *would* be better informed than others who have never even heard of the article (perhaps because they read so slowly that they never got around to it). If one knows of the existence of the article, one can go back and read it more carefully if the need arises.

Brings Useful Material to Your Attention. There is still another advantage in knowing how to skim. People who have the habit of skimming a large amount of material will invariably come across certain articles or parts of books which are of great importance to them. These parts can be read more carefully. But if these readers had never developed the habit of skimming, the chances are that they would never have come across the important parts or articles.

Becoming a More Flexible Reader

If a reader has only one reading speed, it is almost always slow. One mark of poor readers is that they have no rapid reading speed. Good readers have flexibility in their reading. They can go fast when they want to and they can go slowly when they need to.

Skimming is not a skill which should be used at all times or a type of reading which should replace all average or study reading. But it is a skill which can and should be used in many instances. As you become familiar with the technique, you will come to know when you should skim and when you should not. With practice, you will be surprised at the large amount of information you can get by skimming at fast speeds.

The skimming exercises which follow will enable you to develop your ability to skim and help you become a more flexible reader. It is hoped that students using this book will develop control over their reading speed rather than allow their reading speed to control them.

How to Use Part 1: Skimming

1. **Read the Lesson.** Learn what skimming is, when to skim, and how to skim. Reread and review if necessary.

2. **Complete the Practice Exercises.** Apply what was learned in the lesson to the exercises to build skimming skill. Follow these steps.

    a) **Record Skimming Time.** Write down your reading time in the box provided on the first page of each selection. If your instructor is timing the class, follow the instructions given. Convert your time to a words-per-minute rate using the conversion table on page 140. Write your speed in the appropriate box.

    b) **Answer Comprehension Questions.** Answer the questions without looking back. Correct your answers using the key on page 136. Write your score in the appropriate box.

    c) **Record Scores.** Record your comprehension scores and plot your words-per-minute rates for the ten practice exercises on the graph on page 141.

3. **Practice Daily.** Make skimming a regular part of your everyday reading activities.

Skimming Drills

Alexander Dolgun's Story
AN AMERICAN IN THE GULAG

*Alexander Dolgun
with Patrick Watson*

Directions: Skim the selection, looking for main ideas and a few details. When you finish, enter your reading time and speed in the boxes below.

Reading Time ☐

Reading Speed ☐

Comprehension ☐

Sidorov was not in the interrogation room when I got there. I sat on the chair and immediately went to sleep. It probably lasted two minutes, but this time I did not fall off the chair. I was beginning to learn how to sleep in a hard wooden chair without falling off, and to be ready to wake up again at the smallest sound. I had tried it two or three times on Sidorov already but I think he was getting wise to me. He would ask a question and I would say, "Listen, I have to think about that for a minute." Then I would put my hand to my head and close my eyes and doze off, just go to sleep. The first time I came to with a lurch and he knew I had been sleeping. I said, "I can't help it. I'm trying to remember but I'm too sleepy." Sidorov said brusquely, "Keep your eyes open, then." I said, "It helps me to remember. Don't worry, I'll try to stay awake."

I tried it again a day later, in the daytime, and this time I was able to signal myself to wake up in a minute, smoothly, and say quietly, "No, I can't remember," in answer to his question.

This time, as soon as I heard the door opening, I woke up and found I was sitting up straight, and when Sidorov looked at me my eyes were wide open. Sidorov went directly to his big desk opposite my little table and thumped his file folders down on it. He spread out the newspaper and stood over the desk peering at it and wiping something invisible from his trouser leg with the back of his hand. Then he sat down behind the desk and read for a while without looking at me, and pulled a pack of cigarettes out of his pocket and lit one. I recognized the routine. He smoked for a while and then looked at me for quite a long while without speaking. I have talked to hundreds of prisoners who have undergone interrogation, so I know that this is part of an interrogator's method. Keep you waiting and wondering. Sidorov carried it too far with me because he was not a very sensitive man and had no idea what kind of game I was playing. I have *him* wondering, I told myself.

After a while he said, "Prisoner, come over here."

I went and stood in front of his big desk. He had very gray eyes. I noticed that he had missed shaving just under his nose. After a while he offered me a cigarette. "Here."

I took it and he lit it for me with a kind of courtesy.

"Your own are all gone, aren't they?"

"I told you that. Two weeks ago. More. They only lasted two or three days."

"You like to smoke, don't you?"

"Sure I do, you know that."

"I know a lot about you, my friend."

I waited.

"In the labor camp where I will send you when I'm through with you, there is always tobacco, you can have your own and you can smoke whenever you like. Wouldn't that be better than what you're getting here?"

I just smiled my simple smile at him and shrugged.

"Look, prisoner, I'm going to give you some advice. It won't get any better here. You think you're having a hard time, but it can only get harder if you don't cooperate. Now listen, it's all in here anyway"—he slapped the files—"and I'm going to get it out of you because that's my job and I'm good at it and I've never failed yet. So instead of waiting for a month or two or however long you intend to be stubborn, why not get it over with now? Today. Tell me everything because we know it all anyway, all we need is a few details and a signed statement, and then you'll be able to sleep at night and smoke cigarettes and get decent food and be with other people all day long, and you'll probably get a very light sentence for cooperating."

I heard snatches of music running through my head. I laughed out loud and said in English, "Is this the Chattanooga Choo-Choo?"

"What's that?" Sidorov said sharply.

I said, "Why don't you give me a shine?"

"Prisoner, you are forbidden to speak English!"

I said in Russian, "I'm sorry. I'm really sorry. But this is really marvelous! I don't think you realize how marvelous it is."

He said, "What are you getting at?"

I said, "Listen. You're getting extra pay for night interrogations. If I tell you everything right now, you'll lose all those bonuses. Why should I do that to you after all you've done for me? Besides, if you know everything already, what do you need me for anyway? Why not just send me quietly off to camp? You could spend the next six months writing up your reports at home. Then you could report you've got the confession you needed. You don't need me if you know everything."

Being pretty lightheaded, that all sounded better to me than it really was. But it did succeed in confusing Sidorov for a moment. His face was very blank, and then a trace of anger came into it. But he simply turned away without answering and picked up the paper. "You won't feel so witty later tonight," he said tightly.

I drew on the smoke. It went down deliciously and took the top of my windpipe with a satisfying catch. It was the first cigarette since the weekend and it went to my head which was already floating, and made me very relaxed and dying for sleep. I had to fight off an impulse to say to Sidorov, "Please let me go to sleep! If you let me go to sleep, I'll do anything you want."

But there was no point in even trying that because he wanted details of my spying activities and there simply were no spying activities to give him details on. I couldn't win and yet I felt I couldn't lose either, as long as I refused to give in and show any weakness.

All day I sat in the chair, shifting my shrinking buttocks from side to side, trying to blink away the burning in my eyes. Sidorov scarcely spoke. Once or twice he picked up the phone and called his wife. Sometime in the middle of the day he got up and left to get something to eat. He told the guard to make sure I did not go to sleep. I tried sleeping in my chair without showing it, but as soon as the guard saw my eyes closed he came and shook me. The high morale I had built up for myself with songs in the morning was beginning to wear off. I wanted to get back in the cell and sing some more songs, but I knew they shut the wind tunnel down before six o'clock, and I would have to wait until morning. There was a kind of pressure building up inside my skull. Not a headache, just a strong, incessant pressure connected with my eyes. I knew it could only be cured by sleep. Before Sidorov came back I tottered again and fell off the chair with my eyes closed. Somebody picked me up and shook me vigorously.

"Sleep," I said.

"Talk, and you'll get to sleep," Sidorov's voice said. I opened my burning eyes and smiled at him.

Back to the cell at 6 P.M. Sometime in the middle of the day they have brought the midday bowl of thin cabbage soup with a bit of fish in it. When they open the door of cell 111 and shove me in, the soup is sitting there on my plate, cold, and if I want the bit of protein and phosphorous and other essentials it contains, I will have to eat it right away, cold and insipid as it is, or else do without my hot porridge, which will come almost immediately, since I have only one plate.

That night, or one night soon after, two things happened almost simultaneously. I noticed that my hair was falling out, and I found some information on the bottom of my plate.

In fact, my hair had started coming out at the end of the second week. Years later I was told this could be a result of extreme nervous stress, along with everything else that was happening to me. I was losing a lot of weight, but I could afford a bit of that. But there was no fresh food of any kind. I was sure I would start to get scurvy if I stayed in prison very long. My gums were beginning to get sore. When I washed my face and ran some cold water through my hair with my fingers, a few hairs came away and I saw them in the sink. The next time I was taken out for a shower, when I was drying myself, I saw some more hair lying on my arm. This time there was a whole tuft of it. I had brushed my hand across my head to try to ease the pressure in my skull, and I could literally feel a mass of hair come loose as my fingers rubbed my scalp. I brought down a bunch of blond hair and stared at it. The sight of it made me feel quite uneasy. It was a sign of physical decay. I had been expecting something, but not this.

I felt a surge of panic coming on. I said, "Easy, Alex, that's what they want. To make you lose control." I was enormously tempted to feel my head and see if any more hair would come away, but I was terrified that it would, so I didn't. I thought, I've got to get busy at something new, anything to keep my mind active. I tried drawing in deep breaths to see if that would relax me. My chest felt weighted down with hard straps running around my ribs. I got up and ran some more water in the sink and splashed my face with it, and then decided to wash my plate very meticulously and dry it with my little towel. And this is where the information came from.

I remember a story one of the guys at the embassy used to tell, about some guy who went to jail and was criticized by the warden for keeping a pack of cards instead of a Bible in his cell. Then the guy explained to the warden how the cards had a symbolism that reminded him of all the biblical characters and could also function as a calendar and so on. Well, that's what it's like in prison. You make use of the smallest scraps of information and get a lot of mileage from them. When I was drying this enameled metal plate, I noticed on the bottom the name of the Moscow factory where it was made, and the figures 10-22.

I've always enjoyed number games, and I thought, here's one ready made. Figure out what this means, 10-22.

Probably when I first saw those numbers I assumed they were the date of manufacture, October 1922. But the plate was pretty new, not worn enough to be a quarter of a century old. I wondered for a while if it referred to the prison in some kind of code. Then, just while I sat and looked at it in my hand, I found myself saying silently that the plate was about twenty-two centimeters across and the inner section about ten centimeters. If that was true, I could prove it by making some sort of tape measure and checking the two dimensions against each other.

Of course, my belt and tie were gone.

I started looking around the cell for something I could use. The towel caught my eye. It was woven pretty loosely of a fairly coarse cotton. It took just two seconds to unravel a thread from across the end, and I got a piece about forty centimeters long. I broke off a piece a little longer than the width of the plate. I laid it across the diameter of the plate and creased it at what I hoped would be the twenty-two centimeter mark. Then I measured and knotted lengths equal to six centimeters, from the edge to the inner rim; ten centimeters across the inner section; sixteen centimeters from the outer edge right across the inner section; and another of twenty, twice the diameter of the inner section.

I became totally absorbed in this cumbersome arithmetic. From time to time I looked up at the peephole, but what I was doing apparently seemed innocent enough because there was no interruption. Now I measured a thread equal to the difference between the six and the ten, and then folded it in half and found to my delight it was exactly equal to the difference between the twenty and the twenty-two. A small matter, but I almost laughed out loud at my success. All the other comparisons worked. I painstakingly pulled out threads until I had a piece that looked like about a meter, and then divided it up by sharp creases with my teeth into ten ten-centimeter lengths and then divided up the last of these into ten one-centimeter divisions. I now had a ruler.

I at first decided to measure my cell. I said to myself, "I wonder how far I actually walk every day, up and down between these walls?" It was 227 centimeters wide and 351 long. I wondered how many kilometers a day I might make, up and down, up and down, my hands behind my back. I walked from the door to the opposite wall and back. Ten steps, five each way, which meant about seventy centimeters each step. I thought working on a base of seventy might be too much for my mental arithmetic, but if I could shorten the step to 66 $^2/_3$, so that every three steps meant two meters, then a kilometer would take fifteen hundred steps.

I thought, I'll walk to the embassy.

I did not know then precisely where the American Embassy was in relation to Lefortovo Prison, but I remembered that the drive across town in the middle of the night took about fifteen minutes at a pretty modest pace; so I guessed about eight kilometers. Southwest, I guessed. Let's see how long it takes me to get there.

The idea excited me strangely. In my dead black cell, isolated from everyone but the anonymous eye at the peephole every minute or so, the fantasy of a walk across Moscow to join friends was totally seductive. I had not seen the outside of the prison, but I had heard the gates swing open and could imagine their size. I made the gates my first target and got up and started to walk as fast as I could, estimating a slightly shortened pace, and just feeling my way downstairs to the gates. Up and down the cell. Now I am at the corridor of boxes, another thirty steps, lucky the door is open; and no one is looking and I'm out into the courtyard. It's dark enough. There is a van coming in with a prisoner, I'll just slip behind it, and the gates are still open, and out into the snowy streets and freedom!

A nourishing fantasy. An energizing fantasy. I breathed in the clear, cold imaginary air and hugged my coat around me. (What coat? Oh, I had somehow kept the exercise coat; that would do.) I turned southwest and began to count my steps, up and down the cell. I walked past the skating rink, with the lights and music and the boys and girls whirling around, but I didn't look right or left. I just walked and counted, up and down the cell. Now six hundred paces—it will take twelve thousand tonight, Alex old buddy, and you'd better make it by dawn or they'll pick you up. Keep at it.

Now a funny thing happened. I began to recognize the streets of Moscow—streets I'd driven through with the boys from the embassy, out on the town with a borrowed embassy car. I thought, Easy, I can't have come this far. What's the count? Streets I'd driven along with Mary, with her head on my lap, talking about the future, about America, so far to the west.

Now I'm going southwest, in Moscow.

Then I thought, Jesus! Why not go west, not southwest! Why not walk right out of this God-forsaken country? Let's say it's only six kilometers from here to the outskirts of the city proper, then I can pick up a road west and hide in some farm building in the morning and just head right across Russia until I'm free! Only nine thousand paces to the edge of Moscow, kid. Pick it up now, pick it up!

Find out your reading time and enter it in the first box on page 17. Next, turn to page 140 and look up your reading speed (words per minute). Write it in the second box. Then answer the comprehension questions.

Answer these questions without looking back at the selection. Put an _x_ in the box beside the best answer for each question. Try to get 6 correct answers.

1. What is the first indication given to the reader that Alex has been deprived of sleep in prison?
   - ☐ a. Sidorov instructed the guard to make sure Alex did not sleep during Sidorov's breaks.
   - ☐ b. Alex fell asleep as soon as he sat down in the empty interrogation room.
   - ☐ c. Alex was tempted to promise anything in exchange for sleep.

2. What did Alex believe was the purpose of Sidorov's initial behavior in the interrogation room?
   - ☐ a. to make Alex uneasy
   - ☐ b. to see if Alex was awake
   - ☐ c. to give Alex a chance to rest

3. In hopes of getting Alex to talk, Sidorov told him that at the labor camp Alex could have
   - ☐ a. visitor's privileges.
   - ☐ b. medical attention.
   - ☐ c. cigarettes.

4. How did Alex demonstrate his courage upon Sidorov's return to the interrogation room after Alex fell asleep and fell off the interrogation chair?
   - ☐ a. He asked for sleep.
   - ☐ b. He smiled at Sidorov.
   - ☐ c. He spat at Sidorov.

5. What, besides loss of hair, was the sign of physical decay which worried Alex the most?
   - ☐ a. weight loss
   - ☐ b. soreness of the gums
   - ☐ c. scurvy

6. Alex's observation that his hair was falling out led, indirectly, to what important event?
   - ☐ a. He decided to pretend he had scurvy.
   - ☐ b. He discovered where the prison was located.
   - ☐ c. He noticed the numbers on the bottom of his metal plate.

7. The numbers on the bottom of the plate indicated
   - ☐ a. where the plate was made.
   - ☐ b. when the plate was made.
   - ☐ c. the size of the plate.

8. From what did Alex construct his "ruler"?
   - ☐ a. a towel
   - ☐ b. a belt
   - ☐ c. a tie

9. Why was Alex _especially_ excited by the fantasy of walking across Moscow to visit friends?
   - ☐ a. He used to take long walks in Moscow before he was captured.
   - ☐ b. He was becoming irrational and insane.
   - ☐ c. He had been totally isolated from other people in a dark cell.

10. The primary purpose of Alex's plan to walk out of Russia in his imagination was to
    - ☐ a. provide Alex with much-needed exercise.
    - ☐ b. keep Alex's mind active and absorbed.
    - ☐ c. help plan his escape.

Now correct your answers using the Answer Key on page 136. Count the number of correct answers and enter it in the last box on page 17. After you have filled in all three boxes, transfer your reading speed (words per minute) and comprehension score to the Progress Graph on page 141.

To Sir, with Love

E. R. Braithwaite

Directions: Skim the selection, looking for main ideas and a few details. When you finish, enter your reading time and speed in the boxes below.

Reading Time	10:51
Reading Speed	
Comprehension	100%

On Thursday morning the class seemed to be in the grip of some excitement and expectancy. During the recess they stood about the classroom in little whispering groups which fell silent as I approached, but I could read no special significance into this. The lessons proceeded more or less normally, but heavily.

In the afternoon, we went down to the gym for the usual P. T. period. The equipment was neatly arranged around the cleared dining hall; vaulting horse buck, jumping standards, medicine balls, boards, several pairs of boxing gloves slung by their laces across the vaulting horse. The boys were, with one exception, barefoot and wearing only blue shorts. Sapiano sat on a low form, his right arm bandaged from elbow to wrist.

"Line up in the center, will you," I began.

They eagerly obeyed, forming two neat lines. But then Denham stepped forward.

"Please, Sir."

"Yes, Denham?"

"Can't we have boxing today, please, Sir?"

"Why, Denham?"

"Oh, nothing, Sir, just feel we'd like to have a bit of a change, Sir."

"Oh, very well," I replied. "Get into pairs according to size." The pairing was completed in a moment as if by prearrangement, only Denham remained unpaired.

"My partner's crippled, Sir." He indicated the

bandaged Sapiano. "Will you have a go with me?" At this the others, as if on cue, moved quietly toward us, watchful, listening.

"You can wait and have a bout with Potter or one of the others."

The pieces were falling into place, the penny had finally and fatefully dropped.

"They'll be done in, Sir. I don't mind having a knock with you."

"Go on, Sir, take him on."

This chorus of encouragement was definitely not in my best interest. "No, Denham, I think you'll have to skip it for today."

Denham looked at me pityingly, slipped the gloves off his large hands and casually dropped them at my feet. He had made his point. Looking quickly at the others I could read the disappointment and disgust in their faces. They thought I was afraid, scared of the hulking, loutish fellow.

"Okay, let's go." I took a pair of gloves from the horse. Potter stepped over and expertly secured the laces for me while Sapiano, strangely unhampered by his mysterious injury, did the same for Denham. The others meanwhile ranged themselves along the wall, silent and expectant.

As we began to box, it became clear that Denham's reputation as a boxer was thoroughly justified; he was fast and scored easily, though his blows were not delivered with his full weight. I tried to dodge and parry as best I could, being only concerned with riding this out for a little while until I could reasonably stop it. I had stupidly allowed myself to be lured into this one, and it was up to me to extricate myself with as little damage to either dignity or person as I could.

"Come on, Sir, go after him." I recognized Patrick Fernman's voice. Disappointment was poignant in it; they must all be somewhat surprised at my lame efforts.

Suddenly Denham moved in and hit me in the face; the blow stung me and I could feel my eyes filling up with tears; the salt blood in my mouth signalled other damage. I was angry now, this was no longer a pleasant little affair—the fellow meant business. It may have been the sight of blood on my face, or the insistent urging of his cronies to "Go arter 'im;" whatever it was, it spelled Denham's undoing. Guard open, he rushed in and I hit him; my gloved fist sank deep into his solar plexus, and the air sighed out of him as he doubled up and collapsed on the floor.

After a moment of stunned silence, Potter and some others rushed to help him.

"Hold it. Leave him where he is and line up quickly for vaulting. Clarke, collect the gloves and stack them by the door."

To my amazement they obeyed without demur, while I hurried to Denham and helped him over to a low form near the wall; he was only winded and would soon be all right. When he was comfortable I continued with the P. T. lesson, which went without a hitch; the boys were eager to do their best, and went through the movements without recourse to my prompting or direction; they now looked at me as if I had suddenly and satisfactorily grown up before their very eyes.

At the end of the lesson I dismissed the class and went over to Denham; he still looked a bit green.

"That was just a lucky punch, old man; no harm meant. Why don't you pop up to the washroom and soak your head in some cold water? You'll feel a lot better."

"Yes, Sir." His voice was shaky, but there was no hesitation or mimicry about the "Sir." I helped him to his feet and he signalled to Potter, who went off with him toward the washroom.

That incident marked a turning point in my relationship with the class. Gradually Denham's attitude changed, and like it that of his cronies. He could still be depended on to make a wisecrack or comment whenever the opening presented itself, but now these were more acceptable to all of us, for they were no longer made in a spirit of rebellion and viciousness. He appeared clean and more and more helpful and courteous, and with this important area of resistance dispelled the class began to move into high gear. Moreover, I suddenly became aware of an important change in my own relationship to them. I was experiencing more than a mere satisfaction in receiving their attention, obedience, and respect with their acceptance of my position as their teacher. I found myself liking them, really liking them, collectively and singly. At first I had approached each school day a little worried, a little frightened, but mostly determined to make good for the job's sake; now there had occurred in me a new attitude, a concern to teach them for their own sakes, and a deep pleasure at every sign that I had succeeded. It was a delight to be with them, and more and more I had occasion to wonder at their general adult viewpoint. I was learning a little more of them each day. Some of them would remain in the classroom during recess and we'd talk about many things.

They were mostly from large families and understood the need and importance of money;

they even felt that they should already be at work to help ease the financial strain on their parents, and to meet their own increasing demands for clothing, cosmetics, entertainment, etc. They spoke of overcrowding, marriage, and children with casual familiarity; one girl had helped with the unexpected birth of her baby brother, and spoke of it with matronly concern.

The lessons were taking hold. I tried to relate everything academic to familiar things in their daily lives. Weights were related to foodstuffs and fuel, measurements to dress lengths, linoleum, and carpets; in this way they could see the point of it all, and were more prepared to pursue the more abstract concepts. In Geography and History we talked and read, and here I was in the very fortunate position of being able to illustrate from personal experiences. They eagerly participated, asking me questions with a keenness I had not suspected in them, and often the bell for recess, lunch, or the end of the day would find us in the heat of some discussion, disinclined to leave off.

The headmaster would occasionally drop in unexpectedly, and would sometimes find himself drawn into discussions on some point or other; he was pleased, and expressed his satisfaction with my efforts. On one such occasion I mentioned the idea of the visit to the Victoria and Albert Museum.

"I wouldn't advise it," he replied. "You have settled in very nicely with them here, but taking them across London would be another matter entirely."

"I think they'll be okay, Sir."

"There's always a tendency for the best of children to show off when out of the close supervision of the school confines, and these are no exception, they're probably worse than most. After all, you cannot hope to supervise forty-six children by yourself."

"I'd like to try, Sir."

"Out of the question, Braithwaite, but I'll say this. If you can persuade another teacher to go with you, you may. It's entirely against the Council's rules for one teacher to have charge of so many children outside the school."

"I'll see if I can get someone to go with me."

"Fine, if she's agreeable let me know and I'll arrange for a travel warrant."

He was smiling slyly and I wondered who it was he had in mind.

"But what about the teacher's own class, Sir?"

"Don't worry, I'll supervise it for the occasion."

At lunch I mentioned the plan to Miss Blanchard.

"Would you like to help me with them, Miss Blanchard?"

"Gillian."

"Ricky." She smiled. "Well, will you?"

"I'd love to. When do you plan to go?"

"As soon as the headmaster can arrange for the travel warrant."

This was fine.

"Why didn't you ask Miss Clintridge?"

"Just didn't think of it, I suppose."

"Oh." There was playful mockery in those eyes.

When the rest of the staff returned from the dining hall I mentioned the idea of the trip, and that Miss Blanchard had agreed to accompany me. They were, to say the least, very dubious about it. While I sat there listening to them there was a knock on the door. Weston opened it to Patrick Fernman, who asked:

"Please, Sir, Miss Dare would like to know if anyone has fixed the girls' netball."

"Miss Who?" Weston's voice was shrill with astonishment.

"Miss Dare, Sir." Fernman looked at the puzzled face and supplied: "Pamela Dare, Sir."

Without replying Weston walked away from the door to lean against the fireplace, his face a study in exaggerated amazement. I meanwhile took a netball from the sports cupboard and gave it to Fernman, who quickly disappeared, slamming the door in his haste.

"Well, I'll be damned." Weston was smiling, but there was a sneer near the surface of his smile. "Fancy that. 'Miss Dare would like the netball.' " He pointed his pipe at me with a theatrical gesture. "I say, whatever's going on in that classroom of yours, old man? I mean this suburban formality and all. Bit foreign in this neck of the woods, don't you think?"

"Is it really?" I inquired. It had not occurred to me that I would need to defend any improvement in the children's conduct or deportment, and I was not quite sure what Weston was getting at.

"What's it all in aid of, old man?" he continued, his hairy arm stuck out from the seedy, leather-trimmed sleeves like that of a scarecrow; the Wurzel Gummidge of the staffroom. "Some sort of experiment in culture for the millions?"

"Not quite that," I replied. "Just an exercise in elementary courtesy. Does it bother you?" I was becoming irritated by the smile and the unnatural patronizing good humor.

"Bother me? Not at all, old man. But tell me, do you also address them as 'Miss,' or are you exempt because of your, ah, privileged position?"

The rest of the staff were watching us and I felt very uncomfortable.

"I too address the girls as 'Miss'."

"Thoroughly democratic and commendable," he replied, the forced smile becoming even sweeter. "But tell me, are the rest of us uncouth critters expected to follow suit?"

"Not necessarily; it's merely that my class and I have reached an agreement on certain courtesies."

"Thank God for that! I don't somehow see myself addressing those snotty little tarts as 'Miss' along with Denham and Co."

"Is it that you object to being taught a lesson in courtesy by those boys, Mr. Weston?"

I could hardly believe my ears. That was Miss Dawes; I would never have thought of her as coming to anybody's defense, unless it was Miss Phillips's.

"I do not need lessons in manners from those morons—nor from professional virgins either, for that matter."

Miss Dawes blushed, but continued bravely:

"As long as you learn, it doesn't matter who teaches, does it?"

"Good for you, Josy," Clinty interjected.

"Ah, well," Weston resumed, "I suppose it comes natural to some people to say: 'Yes, Ma'am; yes, Boss'."

His caricature of a subservient Negro was so grotesque that I could almost smile. But the intention behind the words was not funny, and I was rather relieved when Grace, with her usual tact, broke into the conversation.

"By the way, Ricky," she called to me, "what have you been saying to Droopy?"

"Droopy? Who or what is Droopy?"

"Oh, come off it. I'm talking about Jane Purcell in your class. You know . . ." and she quoted, "Uncorseted, her friendly bust gives promise, etc., etc."

"Oh, I see. I haven't been saying anything to her specially. Why?"

"All of a sudden she's become very conscious of her, er, mammary glands." Grace's laughter ran round the room until it found reflection in each face there.

"Now she wants advice on the right type of brassiere—I never liked that word, it always sounds like a receptacle for hot coals."

"Could be." Clinty would never be outdone.

"Looks like she chose the right person to advise her." Weston's owl eyes were on Grace's attractive bust; I was sure the untidy fringe around his mouth hid the leer which his voice so clearly revealed.

"A little good advice wouldn't be wasted on you either, my lad." Grace's voice was very frosty now, and Weston shut up.

I felt slightly disturbed by the tensions generated within the staffroom. I had thought that my presence was the red rag to Weston's bull, but now I discovered that his attitude to me was only part of a general situation which had existed for some time before my arrival. Most of the women teachers were obviously fed up at being saddled with a male colleague who never joined in any conversation except to be sarcastic or critical. Gillian, I noticed, remained cool and untroubled by it. She seemed to be able to play the part of observer, letting any discord pass over her, confident in the assurance of her own poise and breeding to keep her inviolate. Miss Phillips seemed unaffected by it for different reasons; she spent her staffroom leisure in some strange world of fancy which was closed to all except Miss Dawes, who also, until today's brave gesture, had never allowed anything which transpired to invade their tight, secret conclave.

But the clash of personalities in the staffroom was, after all, of no great importance, so long as its repercussions did not enter the classrooms. It was the children, not the teachers, who mattered.

Find out your reading time and enter it in the first box on page 22. Next, turn to page 140 and look up your reading speed (words per minute). Write it in the second box. Then answer the comprehension questions.

Answer these questions without looking back at the
selection. Put an *x* in the box beside the best answer for
each question. Try to get 6 correct answers.

1. The narrator of this selection is a
   - ☐ a. social worker.
   - ☒ b. teacher.
   - ☐ c. guidance counselor.

2. By Thursday afternoon, Sir realized that the
   excitement the class had displayed all day was
   caused by
   - ☐ a. the headmaster's promise to take part in
     the day's history discussion.
   - ☐ b. Sir's suggestion that the class visit the
     Victoria and Albert Museum.
   - ☒ c. Denham's plans to maneuver Sir into a
     round of boxing.

3. As the P. T. period progressed, it became clear
   that Sapiano's arm
   - ☐ a. would benefit from exercise.
   - ☒ b. was not really injured.
   - ☐ c. needed further medical attention.

4. In what way did the boxing incident mark a
   turning point in Sir's relationship with the class?
   - ☐ a. The attitudes of Denham and his cronies
     soon became more hostile.
   - ☐ b. Sir realized that his students were, after
     all, only children and began to treat them
     as such.
   - ☒ c. Mutual respect and understanding soon
     grew between Sir and the class.

5. When Sir mentioned his idea of taking his
   students to the Victoria and Albert Museum,
   the headmaster
   - ☒ a. expressed his doubts about the success of
     such a trip.
   - ☐ b. refused to allow Sir to take the students
     on a field trip.
   - ☐ c. felt it was an excellent idea.

6. How many students were in
   Sir's class?
   - ☐ a. 25
   - ☐ b. 33
   - ☒ c. 46

7. Most of Sir's students were from
   - ☒ a. large, poor families.
   - ☐ b. small, middle-class families.
   - ☐ c. large, wealthy families.

8. The custom—newly adopted by Sir's
   students—of using *Miss* when addressing
   female classmates demonstrated the class's
   desire to
   - ☐ a. show Sir how silly the idea was.
   - ☐ b. annoy Weston and other members
     of the faculty.
   - ☒ c. treat each other with courtesy
     and respect.

9. Mr. Weston is best described as
   - ☒ a. fault-finding and rude.
   - ☐ b. nervous and shy.
   - ☐ c. pleasant but quick-tempered.

10. The setting of this passage is
    - ☐ a. America.
    - ☐ b. Canada.
    - ☒ c. England.

**Now correct your answers using the Answer Key
on page 136. Count the number of correct answers
and enter it in the last box on page 22. After you
have filled in all three boxes, transfer your reading speed (words per minute) and comprehension
score to the Progress Graph on page 141.**

Alive

THE STORY OF THE ANDES SURVIVORS

Piers Paul Read

Directions: Skim the selection, looking for main ideas and a few details. When you finish, enter your reading time and speed in the boxes below.

Reading Time	9:41
Reading Speed	
Comprehension	80%

On the morning of the ninth day, the body of Susana Parrado was dragged out onto the snow. No sound but the wind met the ears of the survivors as they stumbled from the cabin; nothing was to be seen but the same monotonous arena of rock and snow.

As the light changed, the mountains took on different moods and appearances. Early in the morning, they seemed bright and distant. Then, as the day progressed, shadows lengthened and the gray, reddish, and green stone became the features of brooding beasts or disgruntled gods frowning down upon the intruders.

The seats of the plane were laid out on the snow like deck chairs on the veranda of an *estancia*. Here, the first out would sit down to melt snow for drinking water while staring at the horizon. Each could see in the face of his companions the rapid progress of their physical deterioration. The movements of those who busied themselves in the cabin or around the fuselage had grown heavy and slow. They were all exhausted by the slightest exertion. Many remained sitting where they had slept, too listless and depressed even to go out into the fresh air. Irritability was an increasing problem.

Marcelo Perez, Daniel Fernandez, and the older members of the group feared that some of the boys were on the verge of hysteria. The waiting was wearing them down. They had started to squabble among themselves.

Marcelo did what he could to set an example. He was optimistic and he was fair. He talked confidently of rescue and tried to get his team to sing songs. There was one desultory rendering of "Clementine," but no one had the spirit to sing. It was also becoming evident to them all that their captain was not as confident as he seemed. At night he was overtaken by melancholy; his mind turned to his mother and how much she must be suffering, to his brother on a honeymoon in Brazil, and to the rest of his family. He tried to hide his sobs from the others, but if he slept he would dream and wake screaming. His friend Eduardo Strauch did his best to comfort him, but Marcelo felt that as captain of the team—and chief exponent of the trip to Chile—he had been responsible for what had happened.

"Don't be a fool," said Eduardo. "You can't look at things like that. I persuaded Gaston and Daniel Shaw to come, and they're both dead. I even rang Daniel to remind him, but I don't feel responsible for his death."

"If anyone's responsible," said his cousin Fito, "it's God. Why did He let Gaston die?" Fito was referring to the fact that Gaston Costemalle, who had fallen out of the back of the plane, was not the first of his family to die; his mother had already lost her husband and other son. "Why does God let us suffer like this? What have we done?"

"It's not as simple as that," said Daniel Fernandez, the third of the Strauch cousins.

There were two or three among the twenty-seven whose courage and example acted as pillars to their morale. Echavarren, in considerable pain from his smashed leg, remained cheerful and outgoing, screaming and cursing at anyone who stepped on him but always making up for it afterward with a courteous apology or a joke. Enrique Platero was energetic and brave, despite the wound in his stomach. And Gustavo Nicolich made his "gang" get up in the morning, tidy the cabin, and then play such games as charades, while at night he persuaded them to say the rosary with Carlitos Paez.

Liliana Methol, the one woman among them, was a unique source of solace. Though younger, at thirty-five, than their mothers, she became for them all an object of filial affection. Gustavo Zerbino, who was only nineteen, called her his godmother, and she responded to him and to the others with comforting words and gentle optimism. She too realized that the boys' morale

was in danger of collapse and thought of ways to distract them from their predicament. On the evening of that ninth day, she gathered them around her and suggested that each tell an anecdote from his past life. Few of them could think of anything to say. Then Pancho Delgado volunteered to tell three stories, all about his future father-in-law.

When he had first met his *novia,* he told them, she was only fifteen, while he was three or four years older. He was not at all sure whether her parents would welcome him, and he was anxious about the impression he would create. Within a short time, Delgado reported, he had accidentally pushed her father into a swimming pool, injuring his leg; he had discharged a shotgun into the roof of their family car, a brand-new BMW 2002, leaving an enormous hole with pieces of metal bent back like the petals of a flower; and he had very nearly electrocuted her father while helping him prepare for a party in the garden of their house in Carrasco.

His anecdotes were like a tonic to the boys sitting in the dank atmosphere of the plane, waiting to feel tired enough to sleep, and for this they felt grateful. Yet when the turn came for other stories, no one spoke, and as the light faded, each returned to his own thoughts.

They awoke on the morning of Sunday, October 22, to face their tenth day on the mountain. First to leave the plane were Marcelo Perez and Roy Harley. Roy had found a transistor radio between two seats and by using a modest knowledge of electronics, acquired when helping a friend construct a hi-fi system, he had been able to make it work. It was difficult to receive signals in the deep cleft between the huge mountains, so Roy made an aerial with strands of wire from the plane's electric circuits. While he turned the dial, Marcelo held the aerial and moved it around. They picked up scraps of broadcasts from Chile but no news of the rescue effort. All that came over the radio waves were the strident voices of Chilean politicians embroiled in the strike by the middle classes against the socialist government of President Allende.

Few of the other boys came out into the snow. Starvation was taking its effect. They were becoming weaker and more listless. When they stood up they felt faint and found it difficult to keep their balance. They felt cold, even when the sun rose to warm them, and their skin started to grow wrinkled like that of old men.

Their food supplies were running out. The daily ration of a scrap of chocolate, a capful of wine, and a teaspoonful of jam or canned fish—eaten slowly to make it last—was more torture than sustenance for these healthy, athletic boys; yet the strong shared it with the weak, the healthy with the injured. It was clear to them all that they could not survive much longer. It was not so much that they were consumed with ravenous hunger as that they felt themselves grow weaker each day, and no knowledge of medicine or nutrition was required to predict how it would end.

Their minds turned to other sources of food. It seemed impossible that there should be nothing whatsoever growing in the Andes, for even the meanest form of plant life might provide some nutrition. In the immediate vicinity of the plane there was only snow. The nearest soil was a hundred feet beneath them. The only ground exposed to sun and air was barren mountain rock on which they found nothing but brittle lichens. They scraped some of it off and mixed it into a paste with melted snow, but the taste was bitter and disgusting, and as food it was worthless. Except for lichens there was nothing. Some thought of the cushions, but even these were not stuffed with straw. Nylon and foam rubber would not help them.

For some days several of the boys had realized that if they were to survive they would have to eat the bodies of those who had died in the crash. It was a ghastly prospect. The corpses lay around the plane in the snow, preserved by the intense cold in the state in which they had died. While the thought of cutting flesh from those who had been their friends was deeply repugnant to them all, a lucid appreciation of their predicament led them to consider it.

Gradually the discussion spread as these boys cautiously mentioned it to their friends or to those they thought would be sympathetic. Finally, Canessa brought it out into the open. He argued forcefully that they were not going to be rescued; that they would have to escape themselves, but that nothing could be done without food; and that the only food was human flesh. He used his knowledge of medicine to describe, in his penetrating, high-pitched voice, how their bodies were using up their reserves. "Every time you move," he said, "you use up part of your own body. Soon we shall be so weak that we won't have the strength even to cut the meat that is lying there before our eyes."

Canessa did not argue just from expediency. He insisted that they had a moral duty to stay alive by any means at their disposal, and because Canessa

was earnest about his religious belief, great weight was given to what he said by the more pious among the survivors.

"It is meat," he said. "That's all it is. The souls have left their bodies and are in heaven with God. All that is left here are the carcasses, which are no more human beings than the dead flesh of the cattle we eat at home."

Others joined the discussion. "Didn't you see," said Fito Strauch, "how much energy we needed just to climb a few hundred feet up the mountain? Think how much more we'll need to climb to the top and then down the other side. It can't be done on a sip of wine and a scrap of chocolate."

The truth of what he said was incontestable.

A meeting was called inside the Fairchild, and for the first time all twenty-seven survivors discussed the issue which faced them—whether or not they should eat the bodies of the dead to survive. Canessa, Zerbino, Fernandez, and Fito Strauch repeated the arguments they had used before. If they did not they would die. It was their moral obligation to live, for their own sake and for the sake of their families. God wanted them to live, and He had given them the means to do so in the dead bodies of their friends. If God had not wished them to live, they would have been killed in the accident; it would be wrong now to reject this gift of life because they were too squeamish.

"But what have we done," asked Marcelo, "that God now asks us to eat the bodies of our dead friends?"

There was a moment's hesistation. Then Zerbino turned to his captain and said, "But what do you think *they* would have thought?"

Marcelo did not answer.

"I know," Zerbino went on, "that if my dead body could help you to stay alive, then I'd certainly want you to use it. In fact, if I do die and you don't eat me, then I'll come back from wherever I am and give you a good kick in the ass."

This argument allayed many doubts, for however reluctant each boy might be to eat the flesh of a friend, all of them agreed with Zerbino. There and then they made a pact that if any more of them were to die, their bodies were to be used as food.

Marcelo still shrank from a decision. He and his diminishing party of optimists held onto the hope of rescue, but few of the others any longer shared their faith. Indeed, a few of the younger boys went over to the pessimists—or the realists, as they considered themselves—with some resentment against Marcelo Perez and Pancho

Delgado. They felt they had been deceived. The rescue they had been promised had not come.

The latter were not without support, however. Coche Inciarte and Numa Turcatti, both strong, tough boys with an inner gentleness, told their companions that while they did not think it would be wrong, they knew that they themselves could not do it. Liliana Methol agreed with them. Her manner was calm as always but, like the others, she grappled with the emotions the issue aroused. Her instinct to survive was strong, her longing for her children was acute, but the thought of eating human flesh horrified her. She did not think it wrong; she could distinguish between sin and physical revulsion, and a social taboo was not a law of God. "But," she said, "as long as there is a chance of rescue, as long as there is *something* left to eat, even if it is only a morsel of chocolate, then I can't do it."

Javier Methol agreed with his wife but would not deter from doing what they felt must be done. No one suggested that God might want them to choose to die. They all believed that virtue lay in survival and that eating their dead friends would in no way endanger their souls, but it was one thing to decide and another to act.

Find out your reading time and enter it in the first box on page 27. Next, turn to page 140 and look up your reading speed (words per minute). Write it in the second box. Then answer the comprehension questions.

**Answer these questions without looking back at the
selection. Put an *x* in the box beside the best answer for
each question. Try to get 6 correct answers.**

1. The survivors obtained drinking water
   ☐ a. from a nearby mountain stream.
   ☒ b. by melting snow.
   ☐ c. from supplies in the plane.

2. Why did Marcelo, the team captain, feel
   responsible for the tragic crash?
   ☒ a. He had been the chief promoter
   of the trip to Chile.
   ☐ b. He had been the copilot.
   ☐ c. He was unable to keep his team's
   morale high.

3. How many people survived the crash?
   ☒ a. 10
   ☐ b. 27 √
   ☐ c. 46

4. Why did Pancho Delgado's future father-in-
   law stories comfort the boys so much?
   ☐ a. Pancho was a great storyteller.
   ☐ b. Most of the boys knew Pancho's
   future father-in-law.
   ☒ c. The stories kept their minds occupied
   for a while.

5. When Roy and Marcelo tried to get a radio to
   work, what were they able to hear?
   ☐ a. news of the rescue effort
   ☒ b. Chilean political broadcasts
   ☐ c. nothing but static

6. Most of the survivors were
   ☐ a. Americans.
   ☐ b. related to each other.
   ☒ c. athletes.

7. The food supplies left from the plane were
   described as "more torture than sustenance"
   for the boys because
   ☐ a. the food was spoiled.
   ☒ b. there was so little food.
   ☐ c. the strong refused to share with
   the weak.

8. Why were they unable to survive on local
   plant life?
   ☒ a. The nearest soil was a hundred feet
   beneath them.
   ☐ b. All available plants were poisonous.
   ☐ c. There was some nourishing plant life,
   but not enough.

9. By the tenth day, most of the survivors
   ☒ a. were too weak to move.
   ☐ b. had given up hope of being rescued. √
   ☐ c. were becoming unruly and violent.

10. How were the more religious survivors able
    to justify cannibalism?
    ☐ a. It was the only practical plan.
    ☒ b. The souls had left the bodies, leaving
    only "meat" behind.
    ☐ c. The survivors didn't know the people
    who had died anyway.

**Now correct your answers using the Answer Key
on page 136. Count the number of correct answers
and enter it in the last box on page 27. After you
have filled in all three boxes, transfer your reading speed (words per minute) and comprehension
score to the Progress Graph on page 141.**

4

Roots

Alex Haley

Directions: Skim the selection, looking for main ideas and a few details. When you finish, enter your reading time and speed in the boxes below.

Reading Time

Reading Speed

Comprehension

With the cutting and piling of the cornstalks at last completed, the "oberseer" began assigning different blacks to a variety of tasks after the conch horn blew each dawn. One morning Kunta was given the job of snapping loose from their thick vines and piling onto a "wagon," as he'd learned they called the rolling boxes, a load of large, heavy vegetables the color of overripe mangoes and somewhat resembling the big gourds that women in Juffure dried out and cut in half to make household bowls. The blacks here called them "punkins."

Riding with the "punkins" on the wagon to unload them at a large building called the "barn," Kunta was able to see that some of the black men were sawing a big tree into thick sections and splitting them with axes and wedges into firewood that children were stacking into long rows as high as their heads. In another place, two men were hanging over thin poles the large leaves of what his nose told him was the filthy pagan tobacco; he had smelled it once before on one of the trips he had taken with his father.

As he rode back and forth to the "barn," he saw that just as it was done in his own village, many things were being dried for later use. Some women were collecting a thick brown "sage-grass," he had heard them call it, and tying it into bundles. And some of the garden's vegetables were being spread out on cloths to dry. Even moss—which had been gathered by groups of children and plunged into boiling water—was being dried as well; he had no idea why.

It turned his stomach to watch—and listen—as he passed a pen where still more swine were being butchered. Their hair, too, he noticed, was being dried and saved—probably for mortar—but the thing that really sickened him was to see the swines' bladders being removed, blown up, tied at the ends, and hung up to dry along a fence; Allah only knew for what unholy purpose.

When he had finished harvesting and storing the "punkins," Kunta was sent with several others to a grove of trees, the limbs of which they were told to shake vigorously so that the nuts growing in them would fall to the ground, where they were picked up by first-kafo children carrying baskets. Kunta picked up one of the nuts and hid it in his clothes to try later when he was alone; it wasn't bad.

When the last of these tasks was done, the men were put to work repairing things that needed it. Kunta helped another man fix a fence. And the women seemed to be busy in a general cleaning of the big white house and their own huts. He saw some of them washing things, first boiling them in a large black tub, then rubbing them up and down against a wrinkled piece of tin in soapy water; he wondered why none of them knew how to wash clothing properly by beating it against rocks.

Kunta noticed that the whip of the "oberseer" seemed to strike down upon someone's back much less often than before. He felt in the atmosphere something similar to the time in Juffure when the harvest had all been put safely into the storehouses. Even before the evening's conch horn would blow to announce the end of the day's work, some of the black men would begin cavorting and prancing and singing among themselves. The "oberseer" would wheel his horse around and brandish his whip, but Kunta could tell he didn't really mean it. And soon the other men would join in, and then the women—singing words that made no sense at all to Kunta. He was so filled with disgust for all of them that he was glad when the conch horn finally signaled for them to return to their huts.

In the evenings, Kunta would sit down sideways just inside the doorway of his hut, heels flat against the packed dirt floor to minimize the iron cuffs' contact with his festering ankles. If there was any light breeze, he enjoyed feeling it blowing against him, and thinking about the fresh carpet of gold and crimson leaves he would find under the trees the next morning. At such times, his mind would wander back to harvest-season evenings in Juffure, with the mosquitoes and other insects tormenting the people as they sat around the smoky night fires and settled into long conversations that would be punctuated now and then by the distant snarling of leopards and the screaming of hyenas.

One night, when Kunta had fallen asleep but drifted again into wakefulness, as he often did, he lay staring up into the darkness and feeling that Allah had somehow, for some reason, *willed* him to be here in this place amid the lost tribe of a great black family that reached its roots back among the ancient forefathers; but unlike himself, these black ones in this place had no knowledge whatsoever of who they were and where they'd come from.

Feeling around him, in some strange way, the presence of his holy-man grandfather, Kunta reached out into the darkness. There was nothing to be felt, but he began speaking aloud to the Alquaran Kairaba Kunta Kinte, imploring him to make known the purpose of his mission here, if there be any. He was startled to hear the sound of his own voice. Up to this moment in the toubob's land, he had never uttered a sound addressed to anyone but Allah, except for those cries that had been torn from him by a lash.

The next morning, as he joined the others in line for the march to work, Kunta almost caught himself saying, "Mornin'," as he had heard them greet each other every day. But though he knew enough toubob words by now not only to understand a good deal of what was said to him but also to make himself somewhat understood as well, something made him decide to continue keeping that knowledge to himself.

It occurred to Kunta that these blacks masked their true feelings for the toubob as carefully as he did his changing attitude toward *them*. He had by now many times witnessed the blacks' grinning faces turn to bitterness the instant a toubob turned his head away. He had seen them break their working tools on purpose, and then act totally unaware of how it happened as the "oberseer" bitterly cursed them for their clumsiness. And he had seen how blacks in the field, for all their show of rushing about whenever the toubob was nearby, were really taking twice as much time as they needed to do whatever they were doing.

He was beginning to realize, too, that like the

Mandinkas' own secret sira kango language, these blacks shared some kind of communication known only among themselves. Sometimes when they were working out in the field, Kunta's glance would catch a small, quick gesture or movement of the head. Or one of them would utter some strange, brief exclamation; at unpredictable intervals another, and then another, would repeat it, always just beyond the hearing of the "oberseer" as he rode about on his horse. And sometimes that told Kunta—even though he couldn't understand it—that some message was being passed, just as the women had done for the men on the big canoe.

When darkness had fallen among the huts and the lamp lights no longer glowed from the windows in the big house, Kunta's sharp ears would detect the swift rustling of one or two blacks slipping away from "slave row"—and a few hours later, slipping back again. He wondered where they were going and for what—and why they were crazy enough to come back. And the next morning in the fields, he would try to guess which of them had done it. Whoever it was, he thought he just might possibly learn to trust them.

Two huts away from Kunta, the blacks would seat themselves around the small fire of the old cooking woman every evening after "supper," and the sight would fill Kunta with a melancholy memory of Juffure, except that the women here sat with the men, and some of both sexes were puffing away on pagan tobacco pipes that now and then glowed dully in the gathering darkness. Listening intently from where he sat just inside his doorway, Kunta could hear them talking over the rasping of the crickets and the distant hooting of owls in the forest. Though he couldn't understand the words, he felt the bitterness in their tone.

Even in the dark, Kunta by now could picture in his mind the face of whichever black was talking. His mind had filed away the voices of each of the dozen adults, along with the name of the tribe he felt that particular one most resembled. He knew which ones among them generally acted more carefree, and which seldom even smiled, a few of them not even around the toubob.

These evening meetings had a general pattern that Kunta had learned. The usual first talker was usually the woman who cooked in the big house. She mimicked things said by both the "massa" and the "missus." Then he heard the big black one who had captured him imitating the "oberseer," and he listened with astonishment as the others all but choked trying to stifle their laughter, lest they be heard in the big white house.

But then the laughter would subside and they would sit around talking among themselves. Kunta heard the helpless, haunted tone of some, and the anger of others, even though he grasped only a little of what they discussed. He had the feeling that they were recalling things that had happened to them earlier in their lives. Some of the women in particular would be talking and then suddenly break into tears. Finally the talking would grow quiet as one of the women began to sing, and the others joined in. Kunta couldn't understand the words—"No-body knows de troubles I'se seed"—but he felt the sadness in the singing.

One thing he didn't hear, it occurred to him, and hadn't heard since he left Africa, was the sound of drums. The toubob probably didn't allow these black people to have any drums; that had to be the reason. But why? Was it because the toubob knew and feared how the sound of the drums could quicken the blood of everyone in a village, until even the little children and the toothless old ones would dance wildly? Or how the rhythm of the drums would drive wrestlers to their greatest feats of strength? Or how the hypnotic beat could send warriors into a frenzy against their enemies? Or perhaps the toubob were simply afraid to allow a form of communication they couldn't understand that could travel the distance between one farm and another.

But these heathen blacks wouldn't understand drumtalk any better than the toubob. Kunta was forced to concede, though—if only with great reluctance—that these pagan blacks might not be totally irredeemable. Ignorant as they were, some of the things they did were purely African, and he could tell that they were totally unaware of it themselves. For one thing, he had heard all his life the very same sounds of exclamation, accompanied by the very same hand gestures and facial expressions. And the way these blacks moved their bodies was also identical. No less so was the way these blacks laughed when they were among themselves—with their whole bodies, just like the people of Juffure.

And Kunta had been reminded of Africa in the way that black women here wore their hair tied up with strings into very tight plaits—although African women often decorated their plaits with colorful beads. And the women of this place knotted cloth pieces over their heads, although they didn't tie them correctly. Kunta saw that even some of these black men wore their hair in short plaits, too, as some men did in Africa.

Kunta also saw Africa in the way that black children here were trained to treat their elders with politeness and respect. He saw it in the way that mothers carried their babies with their plump little legs straddling the mothers' bodies. He noticed even such small customs as how the older ones among these blacks would sit in the evenings rubbing their gums and teeth with the finely crushed end of a twig, which would have been lemongrass root in Juffure. And though he found it difficult to understand how they could do it here in toubob land, Kunta had to admit that these blacks' great love of singing and dancing was unmistakably African.

But what really began to soften his heart somewhat toward these strange people was the fact that over the past moon, their great showing of distaste for him had continued only when the "oberseer" or the "massa" was around. When Kunta came by anywhere the blacks were among themselves, most of them by now would quickly nod, and he would notice their expressions of concern for the worsening condition of his left ankle. Though he always coldly ignored them and hobbled on, he would sometimes find himself later almost wishing that he had returned their nods.

Find out your reading time and enter it in the first box on page 32. Next, turn to page 140 and look up your reading speed (words per minute). Write it in the second box. Then answer the comprehension questions.

Answer these questions without looking back at the selection. Put an *x* in the box beside the best answer for each question. Try to get 6 correct answers.

1. Which activity did Kunta perform in this selection?
   □ a. picking pumpkins
   □ b. splitting trees with an ax
   □ c. drying tobacco leaves

2. Kunta considered the smoking of tobacco to be
   □ a. pagan.
   □ b. beneficial.
   □ c. unhealthy.

3. The slaves exhibited
   □ a. a deep understanding of their African roots.
   □ b. a desire to forget their African roots.
   □ c. no knowledge at all of their African roots.

4. What did Kunta find to be a similarity between the black slaves and the free African blacks he had known?
   □ a. The women washed clothes the same way.
   □ b. The children treated the elders with little respect.
   □ c. Hand gestures and facial expressions seemed the same.

5. You can tell from the selection that Kunta was
   □ a. impressed by customs and practices of the slaves.
   □ b. convinced of the superiority of African ways and customs.
   □ c. not yet aware of differences between the practices of the slaves and those of African blacks.

6. Toubob land means
   □ a. Africa.
   □ b. Juffure.
   □ c. white man's land.

7. The black slaves looked upon Kunta with disfavor
   □ a. only in the presence of white people.
   □ b. all the time.
   □ c. after he had tried to run away.

8. You can infer from the selection that Kunta
   □ a. is a Moslem.
   □ b. is a Christian.
   □ c. follows no religion.

9. Even with his limited command of English, Kunta could tell that the slaves
   □ a. were grateful and loyal to the masters.
   □ b. never dared to admit their feelings of resentment toward the masters.
   □ c. sometimes expressed the contempt they felt for the masters.

10. Kunta's changing attitude toward his fellow slaves can best be described as shifting from
    □ a. utter contempt to understanding.
    □ b. awe to complete disillusionment.
    □ c. hatred to love.

Now correct your answers using the Answer Key on page 136. Count the number of correct answers and enter it in the last box on page 32. After you have filled in all three boxes, transfer your reading speed (words per minute) and comprehension score to the Progress Graph on page 141.

Reincarnation and 13 Pairs of Socks

Jerry Kirshenbaum

Directions: Skim the selection, looking for main ideas and a few details. When you finish, enter your reading time and speed in the boxes below.

Reading Time

Reading Speed

Comprehension

Because of the way he coiled himself in front of the net, goaltender Gary Simmons of the Los Angeles Kings was known as the Cobra. Accordingly, Simmons had a cobra painted on his mask and another tattooed on his right calf. He also wore Stetson hats, Indian bracelets, and a belt fashioned from the skin of a diamondback rattlesnake that he claimed he killed with his bare hands in Arizona one summer. "I guess cobras are quicker than rattlers," he said.

When Dave Dryden played goal for the Buffalo Sabres, he insisted on living in his native Toronto, 100 miles distant. For road games against the Toronto Maple Leafs, Dryden drove to Buffalo, boarded the team bus, and returned to Toronto. After each game he rode the Sabres' bus back to Buffalo, got into his car, and drove home to Toronto. Dryden later played for the Edmonton Oilers, a WHA team 1,700 miles from Toronto. To everyone's immense relief, he lived in Edmonton.

It had been the longtime practice of Minnesota North Star goaltender Gary Smith to undress between periods, laboriously removing his 30 pounds of gear, then putting it all back on again. The reason for this ordeal, Smith once explained, was that his skate boots stretched and he had to remove his equipment to tighten them. And indeed, Smith's boots stretched so much that he had to wear as many as 13 pairs of socks at a time. Finally Smith found boots that kept their shape, and he wore only one pair of socks. No matter. He still undressed between periods.

Ah, the goaltender! Howard Hughes is gone, but as long as hockey clubs find people willing to mind the nets, eccentrics will remain in the public eye. Playing goal, after all, is somewhat bizarre by its very nature, a job that is one of the loneliest in team sports and one of the most harrowing in any business. "It's 60 minutes of hell," said Chico Resch of the New York Islanders.

What makes it hellish, first of all, is that goalies routinely have to fling themselves in front of frozen pucks traveling in excess of 100 mph. Beyond the physical danger is the responsibility of being the last line of defense, where a mistake is often critical and usually highly visible. "You're afraid of getting hurt, but you're even more afraid of being humiliated," Resch once said. "What terrifies me is that we might outplay the other team but that I'll let in a couple of easy goals that cost us the game."

The strain of their job has affected goalies in various ways. In Resch's case, he became slightly manic before games. Driving to one home game, he got so carried away by a song on the radio— Santana's "Black Magic Woman"—that he began banging on the knees of his wife Diane, who had to plead with him to stop. That night he caught himself singing the song aloud in the nets as he shut out Buffalo 3–0. Though Resch credited "Black Magic Woman" for getting "the blood flowing," he was properly remorseful about pounding his wife's knees. "I think I'd be a more relaxed person if I weren't a goaltender," he said.

Resch was spared some of the agonies that have afflicted other goalies, including nervous breakdowns, nervous stomachs, and nervous tics. It is the stuff of legend that Montreal's Wilf Cude, who quit in the early 1940s, did so after throwing a steak at his wife, which persuaded him he was cracking under the pressure. It is also duly chronicled that during his 16-year, 906-game career, Glenn Hall threw up the dressing room before each game and between periods. When Boston's Jim Pettie made his NHL debut, he vomited before and during the game, which Boston won 5–3. Then Pettie got sick again. Finally he faced the reporters. To get the ball rolling, a writer asked, "How do you feel?"

Ask goalies why they willingly subject themselves to such agonies and they concede—and the wording seldom varies—that, "You've got to be crazy to be a goaltender." And the position does attract certain susceptible types: the overweight

kid unable to skate, the younger brother too small to protest, the masochist willing to stand in goal in subzero temperatures while others are darting around the rink. Philadelphia Flyer Coach Fred Shero remembered that he was aghast when his son Rejean announced that he wanted to become a goalie. "I had to do something," Shero said, "so I told him the equipment was too expensive." So Rejean Shero played center on a kids' team, and his father took pleasure in the fact that somebody else's boy played goal.

To cope with the pressures, goalies have resorted to almost anything that might conceivably sharpen the senses or soothe the nerves. Transcendental meditation? Atlanta's Daniel Bouchard meditated regularly to relieve pregame jitters. Resch paid twice-weekly visits to an optometrist for eye-performance exercises that, he insisted, helped him see the puck better. "Most people use only 35% of their visual potential," the Islander goalie said. "The eye muscles can be strengthened like any other muscles." The New York Rangers' Gilles Gratton, who once streaked around the ice when he was playing for the WHA's Toronto Toros, found comfort in his belief in reincarnation. He claimed that in Biblical days he stoned people to death, and he was being repaid with a plague of pucks.

"I was kidding when I said that," Gratton admitted, "but I do think the universe is balanced, and that good and bad are paid back in your later lives." While Gratton was with the Toros he dealt with the here and now by feigning injury to steal breathers during games. When concerned teammates gathered around their fallen goalie, Gratton signaled he was all right by whispering the code words "*poisson mort* (dead fish)."

Because goals are scored on deflections, screens, and jam-ups at the goal mouth just as often as on well-executed plays, it is easy for goalies to conclude that goals are a result of uncontrollable forces, like floods and earthquakes. Accordingly, they can have all sorts of lucky suits, lucky hats, and lucky foods to fend off disaster. The Indianapolis Racers' Andy Brown even had a lucky fan, a middle-aged woman who once fed him lucky cookies and sprigs of heather. Brown could have also used a few rabbits' feet and four-leaf clovers: he was one of the few goalies who continued to play without a mask.

The lengths to which goalies have gone to ward off the evil eye was demonstrated by Vancouver's Cesare Maniago before a home game against the Washington Capitals. Searching his closet for something to wear, Maniago carefully avoided the handsome blue suit he wore the night Boston bombed him 8-1 a few weeks earlier and settled, instead, on a green sport coat and matching slacks, an ensemble he considered luckier than his blue suit. He left so early for the arena that he was the first of his teammates to arrive, assuring him of his lucky parking place. In the locker room Maniago was careful to put his lucky sock, the one with two holes, on his left foot, the same foot on which he wore it during his previous start. He had played well in that game; when Maniago played poorly, he tried to change his fortune by putting the lucky sock on the other foot.

Following these preparations, the thoroughly charmed Maniago performed well in a 5-2 Vancouver win. "I guess having superstitions eases the mind," he said. "You kind of figure if you've done everything exactly right beforehand, nothing much can go wrong when you're on the ice."

Other goalies have gone through similar pregame rituals. For Philadelphia's Gary Innes, these began the night before a game, when he unfailingly took in a movie followed by a chocolate sundae at Howard Johnson's. Buffalo's Gerry Desjardins always took the same route to the rink—and did so even when the city's blizzards made it prudent to try other ways of getting there. In the locker room, Winnipeg's Joe Daley began putting on socks, leg pads, and pants exactly 30 minutes before warmups, then waited precisely 15 more minutes before putting on anything else. Preceding every game, Toronto's Wayne Thomas wrapped his stick with tape; the tape had to be from a brand-new roll and it had to be black.

Many goalies need a pregame perker-upper, which is why Los Angeles' Rogie Vachon always took a whiff of smelling salts and popped a stick of gum into his mouth before leaving the dressing room. His backup man, Simmons, got a lift when he slammed his glove on the top of the door, leaving a dent—the mark of the Cobra?—in every rink in the league. Washington's Bernie Wolfe would not step onto the ice until a stick boy walloped him invigoratingly on the back with a stick. And Toronto's Mike Palmateer gobbled popcorn before he left the Maple Leafs' dressing room.

This sort of thing can continue on the ice. As his teammates whizzed by to wish him luck at the end of warm-ups, a ritual in itself, Toronto's Thomas recited their names aloud, taking pains not to miss anybody. "When they come by three

at a time, it's a test of concentration," he said. After the opening face-off, Boston's Gerry Cheevers liked to bump a rival player—"just to get me into the game." At the end of a period, Atlanta's Bouchard often made a mad dash to the exit. Superstition? Everybody assumed as much, but Bouchard said he just wanted to work up a good sweat going into the dressing room.

The ranks of the ritual-bound also included Montreal's Ken Dryden, who held the NHL's best goals-against average for two consecutive years. Dryden is a lawyer, an ex-member of Nader's Raiders, and an utterly level-headed fellow who never thought of commuting between Toronto and Buffalo, as his brother Dave did. Nevertheless, Dryden took pains to avert his eyes when the referee made his pregame inspection to see if the red goal lights were working. "I just consider it unlucky to see the red light before the game," Dryden once said with a slightly apologetic air. "I know it's silly and I tell myself, 'Ken, you've got to get rid of this bloody superstition.' "

Goaltender superstitions have changed. For years Buffalo's Desjardins drank a lucky pregame cup of coffee. He skipped it before one game and played well anyway. Goodbye, coffee. Like Maniago with his lucky sock, Cleveland's Gilles Meloche made a practice of changing his headband between periods—unless, that is, he had had a hot hand the previous period. During the national anthem, Houston's Ron Grahame stood either at the blue line or in the crease, depending on how things had been going. And Quebec's Serge Aubry disposed of the blue suit that brought him luck when he was with Tulsa in the Central League. It seemed Aubry decided that the luck had gone out of it, so he took the garment to a teammate's back lawn. Aubry and some other players danced around the suit, kicking and spitting on it. Then they poured gasoline on it and sent it up in flames.

Another source of eccentricity are the designs that many goalies have put on their masks. Besides Simmons's cobra, these include star bursts, rebel flags, team insignias, and the snarling lion worn by the Rangers' Gratton, a Leo. Cheevers's mask was considered the acme of the art form. It was decorated with painted stitches depicting the real ones he might have required had he played unprotected. Cheevers began painting his mask in this ghoulish fashion in 1970 and the "stitches" now total over 120.

A mask seems an apt symbol for the goaltender's lonely station in life. For years

Philadelphia's Bernie Parent avoided prying eyes by scrupulously wearing his mask from the moment he left the Flyers' dressing room until the moment he returned. One night, though, Parent lifted his mask during a couple of breaks in the action at a game in Montreal. Afterward, he was asked about the departure. Parent stroked his beard, flashed a smile, and said, "It's because I've gotten better-looking."

Ah, the goaltender! Has there ever been an un-burdened, uncomplicated one in the bunch? Well, yes, there has been. His name was Pete LoPresti, a second-generation goalie (his dad, Sam, played briefly for the Chicago Black Hawks just before World War II) who shared Minnesota's nets with Gary Smith of 13-pairs-of-socks fame. A native of Eveleth, Minnesota, LoPresti was a tough-minded sort, as he demonstrated when the Canadiens came to town in his rookie season, needing five goals to give them a total of 10,000 in their history. After Montreal shellacked Minnesota and LoPresti 7–2, a reporter said, "Do you feel bad about letting the Canadiens reach that milestone, Pete?"

"Why should I?" LoPresti replied. "They've scored more than 10,000 goals and I only gave up seven of them."

LoPresti had no superstitions and no quirks. When he walked the eight blocks from his apartment to the North Stars' Metropolitan Center, he took the shortest route, not a lucky one. To the despair of his wife Terese, the only pregame food he wanted was whatever he found in the refrigerator; before one game he dined on a bologna sandwich and a glass of milk. Nor did LoPresti waste too much time bemoaning the goaltender's lot.

"In a sense a goalie's job is simple," he said. "It's to keep the puck out, nothing more. A defenseman has to skate, stop two-on-one breaks, and sometimes block shots. We're protected and they're not. Of course, a lot of goalies don't look at it that way." LoPresti allowed a trace of mock anxiety to creep into his voice. "I see these other goalies with all their superstitions and illnesses and I wonder why I'm not that way. I mean, is there something wrong with *me?*"

Find out your reading time and enter it in the first box on page 37. Next, turn to page 140 and look up your reading speed (words per minute). Write it in the second box. Then answer the comprehension questions.

COMPREHENSION

Answer these questions without looking back at the selection. Put an *x* in the box beside the best answer for each question. Try to get 6 correct answers.

1. Gary Simmons of the Los Angeles Kings was known as the Cobra because he
   - ☐ a. wore a snake bracelet.
   - ☐ b. coiled himself around the net in a snake-like way.
   - ☐ c. killed a rattlesnake with his bare hands.

2. How many pounds of gear do some goalies wear?
   - ☐ a. 15 pounds
   - ☐ b. 30 pounds
   - ☐ c. 45 pounds

3. According to the article, goalies are afraid of being hurt but they are even more afraid of being
   - ☐ a. fired.
   - ☐ b. taken out of the game.
   - ☐ c. humiliated.

4. According to the article, goalies say that they willingly subject themselves to the terrible strains of playing their position because they
   - ☐ a. use the least expensive equipment.
   - ☐ b. are "crazy."
   - ☐ c. can't skate fast enough to play other positions.

5. Which activity was mentioned in the article as a way to handle the anxieties of goalies?
   - ☐ a. transcendental meditation
   - ☐ b. fishing
   - ☐ c. vigorous exercise

6. Why, according to the article, do goalies tend to rely on "lucky" symbols?
   - ☐ a. The job itself tends to attract superstitious people.
   - ☐ b. Most goalies lack confidence in themselves.
   - ☐ c. Some goalies have concluded that goals are often the result of uncontrollable forces.

7. Which response below was mentioned as a pregame ritual?
   - ☐ a. getting up on the left side of the bed the morning before the game
   - ☐ b. whistling the same song before every game
   - ☐ c. gobbling popcorn before every game

8. Which lucky symbol was burned by a goalie and his teammates?
   - ☐ a. a sock
   - ☐ b. a headband
   - ☐ c. a suit

9. Which mask design was considered to be the height of the goalie mask art form?
   - ☐ a. a cobra
   - ☐ b. painted stitches
   - ☐ c. a snarling lion

10. The goalie who seemed to be free of superstitions was
   - ☐ a. Gary Smith.
   - ☐ b. Cesare Maniago.
   - ☐ c. Pete LoPresti.

Now correct your answers using the Answer Key on page 136. Count the number of correct answers and enter it in the last box on page 37. After you have filled in all three boxes, transfer your reading speed (words per minute) and comprehension score to the Progress Graph on page 141.

Sharks: The Silent Savages

Theo W. Brown

Directions: Skim the selection, looking for main ideas and a few details. When you finish, enter your reading time and speed in the boxes below.

Reading Time

Reading Speed

Comprehension

The sharks considered dangerous to man have to be divided into two classes, the known man-eaters and the reputed man-eaters. The known man-eating species of shark are few. Of these, the white shark *(Carcharodon carcharias)* is the most ferocious and dangerous known to man. Often called by Australians the white pointer, this shark is also known throughout the rest of the world under a variety of names which include the white death, the great white shark, the grey shark, the grey death, and the grey pointer. Without a doubt this is the most terrible monster the seas have produced in recent times. It has been recorded to be a length of almost 40 feet, with a specimen of 39½ feet being captured off the Hawaiian Islands in the late 1930s, and another estimated at 36½ feet in length at Port Fairy in Victoria. Such an animal must have weighed several tons or more. The white shark is found in every ocean and sea of the world. It is most prolific in cooler waters, although still common and often encountered in tropical and semitropical regions.

Since men first took to the sea in ships, the white shark has been known and feared, instilling terror into the hardiest of sailors. Perhaps the "ghostly" white appearance of this huge shark has earned it its evil reputation, for there is something unreal and sinister about the great beast. The white shark has been known to follow sailing vessels for days, even weeks, gliding silently near the keel or close to the stern, watching and waiting. It has been recorded in the old sailing days that the hungry monster has reached out of the ocean to snatch some helpless seaman from the side of his becalmed ship.

On the few occasions when I have encountered this terrible animal under water, I have always been impressed by its unnatural appearance. It has a huge, unblinking black eye and is easily identified by its mackerel-shaped tail—in fact, the family Isuridae which comprises the white shark and its near relative the blue pointer or mako shark *(Isurus glaucus)*, also a reputed man-eater, are often known as mackerel sharks. It has been said that if a diver comes face to face with a white shark this is the last thing he will ever see. But like the lion, the Lord of the Jungle, these sharks have been known to turn and flee in terror at the sight of a man under water. It is enough to know that this huge beast attacks without provocation and without warning and that it has devoured many of the hapless victims of disasters at sea. It is fortunate that the white shark is a pelagic species, roaming the deep ocean waters of the world and only rarely entering the shallow waters of our coastal regions. There is a recorded case of one of the old sailing clippers being attacked repeatedly by this huge animal while moving through the sea. When, a few weeks later, the vessel was run onto the slip for careening, there, embedded deeply in the timbers, having penetrated the stout copper sheathing, was the entire jaw of a white shark. So furious had been the animal's attack and so powerful its bite that it had been unable to withdraw its teeth.

The white shark is the only shark that appears to be capable of a basic and limited reasoning. It is the only shark that will retaliate immediately if molested or injured, its other relatives usually showing a desire to escape rather than attack. When I have captured these huge animals on the massive set rig employed for the pelagic sharks, I have seen them attack and sink the 44-gallon drums used as marker buoys. When brought alongside, they have attacked the side of the boat. On one occasion an angry white shark smashed the divers' platform on the stern of the boat to splintered matchwood, all the time making the most terrible growling and grunting noises.

Another known man-eater is the whaler shark *(Carcharhinus leucas)*, which is the species responsible for the majority of attacks in Australian waters. A friend of mine, Professor Jack Garrick of the Wellington University, New Zealand, and a world authority on sharks, has discovered in recent years that the dangerous Zambesi shark of South Africa, the feared bull shark of the United States, and the species responsible for human attacks in the Tigris and Euphrates rivers and in the Ganges and other rivers and streams of India and Pakistan, is none other than *Carcharhinus leucas*. And the aggressive freshwater sharks of Lake Nicaragua and Lake Izabal in Guatemala, as well as at least one lake in New Guinea, are also whaler sharks. This dangerous animal inhabits close inshore waters, including tidal harbors, rivers, streams, creeks, and estuaries, where its favorite haunts include brackish backwaters. It lurks in the often turbid water, unseen, but an ever-present menace. It was a shark of this species that fatally mauled Ken.

Growing to a length of around 14 to 15 feet, this shark is often found in regions of completely fresh water, so far does it move upstream from the sea and tidal influence. During experimental work with the whaler shark and its close relative, the bronze whaler *(Carcharhinus ahenea)*, I have found that these animals must be treated with extreme caution and respect. Although the bronze whaler is reputed to be a man-eating shark, the largest of this species I have ever encountered was around 7½ to 8 feet in length. Certainly the animal is a very lively one, and also a very beautiful one when observed in its natural habitat. Unlike the whaler shark, the bronze whaler is to be found only in the clear open sea of the coastal regions. Its bright bronze coloring, lightening to a pure white underneath the body, is very attractive to behold.

Another of the known man-eating sharks that has earned its evil reputation around the entire globe is the tiger *(Galeocerdo cuvieri)*. More common in the tropical and subtropical regions than in cooler waters, these sharks are universally known and feared. Estimated to reach a size of at least 30 feet, this species is identifiable when seen under water by the distinctive stripes that have earned it the name of "tiger." These stripes become less noticeable as the shark grows larger, and the markings tend to blend in with the surrounding coloring. Even in a small shark they fade quickly after death. The species was tentatively identified as the one responsible for the fatal mauling of Robert Bartle, 23 years old, of Perth, when he was bitten completely in half while spearfishing in clear waters north of Jurien Bay during August 1967. The shark, previously unseen by the victim or his companion witness, suddenly rushed upon Bartle and seized his body in its jaws, severing it at a point inches below the rib cage and swallowing the buttocks and legs whole. The horrified witness to this terrible incident was Lee Warner of Perth. He told of seeing the attacking shark's eye roll white, as if it was covered with white skin, when the animal flashed past him. In this Warner would have been referring to the nictitating membrane, which is sometimes called a third eyelid. This is a protective whitish membrane of tough skin that slides up over the eye of the shark when it attacks. Not all species have this. It is absent in the white shark, but the tiger shark has it. This evidence, together with an examination of the later-recovered upper portion of the body, which revealed even teeth marks on the upper and lower surfaces corresponding to the upper and lower jaws of the shark, tentatively established that a tiger shark had been responsible for Bartle's death.

These three species are the most dangerous man-eaters known and are responsible for the majority of attacks and fatalities throughout the oceans of the world.

Included among the suspect sharks, or reputed man-eaters, are the larger hammerheads, including *Sphyrna lewini,* with their oddly shaped heads and widely separated eyes and the great blue shark *(Prionace glauca),* another of the deep water or pelagic species. In the United States the lemon shark *(Negaprion brevirostris),* the dusky shark *(Carcharhinus obscurus)* and the oceanic white-tip shark *(Carcharhinus longimanus)* are all considered dangerous.

The famed grey nurse *(Carcharias taurus)* must be mentioned, too. This shark has been credited, although unjustly, by the Australian press with more attacks on humans than any other species. Perhaps there is something sinister in the name "grey nurse" which excites public interest. I have found the animal to be extremely docile and lethargic if left alone and unmolested, though it certainly has a frightening appearance, with a hideous array of long, awl-like teeth protruding from its ferocious-looking jaws. Generally, if approached quietly, it is too lazy to move off the sea floor where it appears to spend much of its life. There is no evidence that a grey nurse shark has ever been involved in an attack on a human. But, as with all marine animals I encounter, I treat this one with the caution and respect it deserves.

A few of the harmless sharks warrant a mention, and these include the whale or checker-board shark *(Rhincodon typus),* which reaches the estimated length of a staggering 70 or 75 feet. This huge and gentle creature roams the oceans feeding on the plankton and minute fishes that nourish its enormous bulk. Another "monster" with an equally gentle disposition is the basking shark *(Cetorhinus maximus),* which also feeds on plankton and has been known to exceed 40 feet in length. Occasionally one of these huge sharks will be rammed by a passing steamer as it lazily moves about in the warm surface layers of the ocean.

Another shark of interest is the thresher shark *(Alopias vulpinus)* with its beautifully fashioned tail. This perhaps is one of the easiest sharks to recognize, since the upper lobe of the tail is as long if not longer than the rest of the body.

The unusual six and seven gilled sharks (most sharks have only five gill openings) I have seen in the shallow waters of a lagoon in the Central and South Pacific, but they appear to prefer the deeper waters of the ocean.

The many beautiful and often delicately marked reef species are ever present. They include the wobbegong or carpet sharks, their multi-patterned bodies blending in with the surrounding environment to make them difficult to detect. These sharks are so fond of crayfish that they will actually enter a cray-pot to obtain these succulent marine delicacies. In western Australia I once found a seven-foot specimen inside one of my standard cane cray-pots. So large was the "wobby" that it occupied the entire inside of the pot, and it is still a mystery how it fitted itself down the narrow neck. I had to dismantle the pot to free the shark, which was later eaten with relish by members of my party.

The white-tipped and black-tipped reef sharks, and the beautiful little epaulette shark, are just some of the host of wonderful animals that make up part of the family of sharks.

Sharks are of extreme benefit to mankind as a source of food, and anyone who has bought cooked fish or eaten it in a restaurant has no doubt eaten, and enjoyed, shark flesh. In Perth an experiment was conducted with the prepared flesh of several of the best eating fish, including jewfish and snapper as well as shark flesh. It was cooked in various ways and presented, with a numbered identification marking only, to the gourmets who were participating in the experiment. None of those who ate the prepared flesh could distinguish between the other fish and the shark. The Chinese are fond of shark-fin soup made from the sun-dried fins, and shark hide is much in demand because it makes tough and good-looking leather from which to make shoes and boots, wallets, golf bags, luggage, watchbands, and dozens of other useful objects. At one time the liver of sharks was much sought after because of its high vitamin A content, and many fishermen were made rich through shark fishing before the introduction of synthetic vitamin A put an end to the market.

Find out your reading time and enter it in the first box on page 42. Next, turn to page 140 and look up your reading speed (words per minute). Write it in the second box. Then answer the comprehension questions.

Answer these questions without looking back at the selection. Put an x in the box beside the best answer for each question. Try to get 6 correct answers.

1. The white shark, the most ferocious and dangerous shark known to man, can be found
   - ☑ a. in every ocean and sea.
   - ☐ b. only in cooler waters.
   - ☐ c. most often in semitropical regions.

2. Like the lion, the white shark will
   - ☐ a. always attack a man if they meet face-to-face.
   - ☑ b. rarely attack a man if they meet face-to-face.
   - ☐ c. occasionally flee at the sight of a human face-to-face.

3. According to the article, the white shark is a "pelagic" species which roams
   - ☐ a. mainly shallow coastal waters.
   - ☐ b. equally over deep and coastal waters.
   - ☐ c. mainly the deep ocean waters.

4. Except for the white shark, most sharks
   - ☐ a. retaliate immediately if molested.
   - ☐ b. show a desire to escape if molested.
   - ☐ c. appear capable of a basic and limited reasoning.

5. The whaler shark, a known man-eater like the white shark, is especially dangerous to man because it
   - ☐ a. attacks whales.
   - ☐ b. is as large as a whale.
   - ☐ c. inhabits close inshore waters.

6. The most unusual thing about the stripes of tiger sharks is that they
   - ☐ a. become more noticeable as the shark grows larger.
   - ☐ b. fade quickly after death.
   - ☐ c. become even more noticeable after death.

7. What do the tiger shark, white shark, and whaler shark all have in common?
   - ☐ a. They all have distinctive stripes.
   - ☐ b. They are responsible for most shark attacks and fatalities.
   - ☐ c. They are all characterized by the nictitating membrane.

8. According to the article, the grey nurse has been blamed by the Australian press for so many attacks on humans because
   - ☐ a. it has attacked more humans than all other sharks combined.
   - ☐ b. it is often confused with the whaler shark.
   - ☐ c. its sinister name excites public interest.

9. It can be concluded from this article that
   - ☐ a. there are some species of sharks which are harmless.
   - ☐ b. there are no harmless sharks.
   - ☐ c. only the wobbegong shark is harmless.

10. According to this selection, the greatest benefit of sharks to mankind is as
    - ☐ a. the only source of vitamin A.
    - ☐ b. a source of leather.
    - ☐ c. a source of food.

Now correct your answers using the Answer Key on page 136. Count the number of correct answers and enter it in the last box on page 42. After you have filled in all three boxes, transfer your reading speed (words per minute) and comprehension score to the Progress Graph on page 141.

My Early Life

Winston S. Churchill

Directions: Skim the selection, looking for main ideas and a few details. When you finish, enter your reading time and speed in the boxes below.

Reading Time

Reading Speed

Comprehension

I had scarcely passed my twelfth birthday when I entered the inhospitable regions of examinations, through which for the next seven years I was destined to journey. These examinations were a great trial to me. The subjects which were dearest to the examiners were almost invariably those I fancied least. I would have liked to have been examined in history, poetry, and writing essays. The examiners, on the other hand, were partial to Latin and mathematics. And their will prevailed. Moreover, the questions which they asked on both these subjects were almost invariably those to which I was unable to suggest a satisfactory answer. I should have liked to be asked to say what I knew. They always tried to ask what I did not know. When I would have willingly displayed my knowledge, they sought to expose my ignorance. This sort of treatment had only one result: I did not do well in examinations.

This was especially true of my entrance examination to Harrow. The headmaster, Dr. Welldon, however, took a broad-minded view of my Latin prose: he showed discernment in judging my general ability. This was the more remarkable, because I was found unable to answer a single question in the Latin paper. I wrote my name at the top of the page. I wrote down the number of the question "I." After much reflection I put a bracket round it thus "(I)." But thereafter I could not think of anything connected with it that was either relevant or true. Incidentally there arrived from nowhere in particular a blot and several smudges. I gazed for two whole hours at this sad spectacle: and then merciful ushers collected my piece of foolscap with all the others and carried it up to the headmaster's table. It was from these slender indications of scholarship that Dr. Welldon drew the conclusion that I was worthy to pass into Harrow. It is very much to his credit. It showed that he was a man capable of looking beneath the surface of things: a man not dependent upon paper manifestations. I have always had the greatest regard for him.

In consequence of his decision, I was in due course placed in the third, or lowest, division of the Fourth, or bottom, Form. The names of the new boys were printed in the School List in alphabetical order; and as my correct name, Spencer-Churchill, began with an "S," I gained no more advantage from the alphabet than from the wider sphere of letters. I was in fact only two from the bottom of the whole school; and these two, I regret to say, disappeared almost immediately through illness or some other cause.

The Harrow custom of calling the roll is different from that of Eton. At Eton the boys stand in a cluster and lift their hats when their names are called. At Harrow they file past a master in the school yard and answer one by one. My position was therefore revealed in its somewhat invidious humility. It was the year 1887, Lord Randolph Churchill had only just resigned his position as Leader of the House of Commons and Chancellor of the Exchequer, and he still towered in the forefront of politics. In consequence large numbers of visitors of both sexes used to wait on the school steps, in order to see me march by; and I frequently heard the irreverent comment, "Why, he's last of all!"

I continued in this unpretentious situation for nearly a year. However, by being so long in the lowest form I gained an immense advantage over the cleverer boys. They all went on to learn Latin and Greek and splendid things like that. But I was taught English. We were considered such dunces that we could learn only English. Mr. Somervell —a most delightful man, to whom my debt is great—was charged with the duty of teaching the stupidest boys the most disregarded thing— namely, to write mere English. He knew how to do it. He taught it as no one else has ever taught it. Not only did we learn English parsing thoroughly, but we also practiced continually English analysis.

Mr. Somervell had a system of his own. He took a fairly long sentence and broke it up into its components by means of black, red, blue, and green inks. Subject, verb, object: Relative Clauses, Conditional Clauses, Conjunctive and Disjunctive Clauses! Each had its color and its bracket. It was a kind of drill.

We did it almost daily. As I remained in the Third Fourth three times as long as anyone else, I had three times as much of it. I learned it thoroughly. Thus I got into my bones the essential structure of the ordinary British sentence—which is a noble thing. And when in after years my schoolfellows who had won prizes and distinction for writing such beautiful Latin poetry and pithy Greek epigrams had to come down again to common English, to earn their living or make their way, I did not feel myself at any disadvantage. Naturally I am biased in favor of boys learning English. I would make them all learn English: and then I would let the clever ones learn Latin as an honor, and Greek as a treat. But the only thing I would whip them for would be for not knowing English. I would whip them hard for that.

I first went to Harrow in the summer term. The school possessed the biggest swimming bath I had ever seen. It was more like the bend of a river than a bath, and it had two bridges across it. Thither we used to repair for hours at a time and bask between our dips eating enormous buns on the hot asphalt margin. Naturally it was a good joke to come up behind some naked friend, or even enemy, and push him in. I made quite a habit of this with boys of my own size or less.

One day when I had been in school about a month, I saw a boy standing in a meditative posture wrapped in a towel on the very brink. He was no bigger than I was, so I thought him fair game. Coming stealthily behind I pushed him in, holding on to his towel out of humanity, so that it should not get wet. I was startled to see a furious face emerge from the foam, and a being evidently of enormous strength making its way by fierce strokes to the shore. I fled, but in vain. Swift as the wind my pursuer overtook me, seized me in a ferocious grip, and hurled me into the deepest part of the pool. I soon scrambled out on the other side, and found myself surrounded by an agitated crowd of younger boys. "You're in for it," they said. "Do you know what you have done? It's Amery, he's in the Sixth Form. He is Head of his House; he is champion at Gym, he has got his football colors."

They continued to recount his many titles to

fame and reverence and to dilate upon the awful retribution that would fall upon me. I was convulsed not only with terror, but with the guilt of sacrilege. How could I tell his rank when he was in a bath towel and so small? I determined to apologize immediately. I approached the potentiate in lively trepidation. "I am very sorry," I said. "I mistook you for a Fourth Form boy. You are so small." He did not seem at all placated by this; so I added in a most brilliant recovery, "My father, who is a great man, is also small." At this he laughed, and after some general remarks about my "cheek" and how I had better be careful in the future, signified that the incident was closed.

I have been fortunate to see a good deal more of him, in times when three years' difference in age is not so important as it is at school. We were afterwards to be Cabinet colleagues for a good many years.

It was thought incongruous that while I apparently stagnated in the lowest form, I should gain a prize open to the whole school for reciting to the headmaster twelve hundred lines of Macaulay's "Lays of Ancient Rome" without making a single mistake. I also succeeded in passing the preliminary examination for the Army while still almost at the bottom of the school. This examination seemed to have called forth a very special effort on my part, for many boys far above me in the school failed in it. I also had a piece of good luck. We knew that among other questions we should be asked to draw from memory a map of some country or other. The night before by way of final preparation I put the names of all the maps in the atlas into a hat and drew out New Zealand. I applied my good memory to the geography of that Dominion. Sure enough the first question in the paper was: "Draw a map of New Zealand." This was what is called at Monte Carlo an *en plein,* and I ought to have been paid thirty-five times my stake. However, I certainly got paid very high marks for my paper.

I was now embarked on a military career. This orientation was entirely due to my collection of soldiers. I had ultimately nearly fifteen hundred. They were all of one size, all British, and organized as an infantry division with a cavalry brigade. My brother Jack commanded the hostile army. But by a Treaty for the Limitation of Armament he was only allowed to have black troops, and they were not allowed to have artillery. Very important! I could muster myself only eighteen field guns—besides fortress pieces. But all the other services were complete—except

one. It is what every army is always short of— transport. My father's old friend, Sir Henry Drummond Wolff, admiring my array, noticed this deficiency and provided a fund from which it was to some extent supplied.

The day came when my father himself paid a formal visit of inspection. All the troops were arranged in the correct formation of attack. He spent twenty minutes studying the scene—which was really impressive—with a keen eye and captivating smile. At the end he asked me if I would like to go into the Army. I thought it would be splendid to command an Army, so I said "yes" at once, and immediately I was taken at my word. For years I thought my father with his experience and flair had discerned in me the qualities of military genius. But I was told later that he had only come to the conclusion that I was not clever enough to go to the Bar. However that may be, the toy soliders turned the current of my life. Henceforward all my education was directed to passing into Sandhurst and to the technical details of the profession of arms. Anything else I had to pick up for myself.

I spent nearly four and a half years at Harrow, of which three were in the Army class. To this I was admitted in consequence of having passed the preliminary examination. It consisted of boys of the middle and higher forms of the school and of very different ages, all of whom were being prepared either for the Sandhurst or the Woolwich examination. We were withdrawn from the ordinary movement of the school from form to form. In consequence I got no promotion or very little and remained quite low down upon the school list, though working alongside of boys nearly all in the Fifth Form.

Meanwhile I found an admirable method of learning my Latin translations. I was always very slow at using a dictionary; it was just like using a telephone directory. It is easy to open it more or less at the right letter, but then you have to turn backwards and forwards and peer up and down the columns and very often find yourself three or four pages the wrong side of the word you want. In short I found it laborious, while to other boys it seemed no trouble.

But now I formed an alliance with a boy in the Sixth Form. He was very clever and could read Latin as easily as English. Caesar, Ovid, Virgil, Horace, and even Martial's epigrams were all the same to him. My daily task was perhaps ten or fifteen lines. This would ordinarily have taken me an hour or an hour and a half to decipher, and then it would probably have been wrong. But my friend could in five minutes construe it for me word by word, and once I had seen it exposed, I remembered it firmly.

My Sixth-Form friend for his part was almost as much troubled by the English essays he had to write for the headmaster as I was by these Latin crossword puzzles. We agreed together that he should tell me my Latin translations and that I should do his essays. The arrangement worked admirably. The Latin master seemed quite satisfied with my work, and I had more time to myself in the mornings. On the other hand once a week or so I had to compose the essays of my Sixth-Form friend. I used to walk up and down the room dictating—just as I do now—and he sat in the corner and wrote it down in longhand.

For several months no difficulty arose; but once we were nearly caught out. One of these essays was thought to have merit. It was "sent up" to the headmaster who summoned my friend, commended him on his work, and proceeded to discuss the topic with him in a lively spirit. "I was interested in this point you make here. You might I think have gone even further. Tell me exactly what you had in your mind." Dr. Welldon, in spite of very chilling responses, continued in this way for some time to the deep consternation of my confederate. However the headmaster, not wishing to turn an occasion of praise into one of cavilling, finally let him go with the remark "You seem to be better at writing than at oral work." He came back to me like a man who has had a very narrow squeak, and I was most careful ever afterwards to keep to the beaten track in essay writing.

Find out your reading time and enter it in the first box on page 47. Next, turn to page 140 and look up your reading speed (words per minute). Write it in the second box. Then answer the comprehension questions.

**Answer these questions without looking back at the
selection. Put an *x* in the box beside the best answer for
each question. Try to get 6 correct answers.**

1. According to this selection, which were
   Churchill's favorite subjects?
   ☐ a. Latin and mathematics
   ☐ b. Greek, poetry, and history
   ☐ c. history, poetry, and writing essays

2. How did Churchill rate his general
   performance on examinations?
   ☐ a. He did extremely well.
   ☐ b. He did not do well.
   ☐ c. He refused to take examinations.

3. The large number of visitors who used
   to wait on the school steps to see Churchill
   march by were surprised to learn that
   he was
   ☐ a. so small.
   ☐ b. first in his form.
   ☐ c. the last one of all.

4. What great advantage did Churchill
   find in his prolonged placement in the
   lowest form?
   ☐ a. He achieved an excellent command
        of Latin and Greek.
   ☐ b. He achieved an excellent command
        of the English language.
   ☐ c. He achieved an excellent command
        of military strategy.

5. What role did Amery, the older boy
   Churchill pushed into the pool, play in
   Churchill's later life?
   ☐ a. They were Cabinet colleagues
        together.
   ☐ b. They played football together.
   ☐ c. They were in the army together.

6. Why did Churchill do so well on the portion
   of the army examination which involved
   drawing a map of New Zealand?
   ☐ a. It was pure luck.
   ☐ b. It was a combination of luck and effort.
   ☐ c. He cheated on the exam.

7. According to Churchill, his inclination
   toward a military career came as a direct
   result of his
   ☐ a. father's military career.
   ☐ b. brother's advice.
   ☐ c. collection of toy soldiers.

8. Why did Churchill's father encourage him to
   go into the military?
   ☐ a. He discerned in Churchill a budding
        military genius.
   ☐ b. He thought his son was not bright
        enough to go to the Bar.
   ☐ c. He had loved army life himself.

9. What kind of alliance did Churchill work out
   with a fellow student?
   ☐ a. His friend told him Latin translations,
        while he dictated the other boy's essays.
   ☐ b. He did his friend's Latin translations,
        and the other boy wrote his essays.
   ☐ c. He taught the other boy to swim in
        return for Latin translations.

10. It is likely that Churchill's great skill
    as a speaker can be attributed in large
    extent to his
    ☐ a. army training.
    ☐ b. rigorous training in English grammar.
    ☐ c. skills in Latin.

**Now correct your answers using the Answer Key
on page 136. Count the number of correct answers
and enter it in the last box on page 47. After you
have filled in all three boxes, transfer your reading speed (words per minute) and comprehension
score to the Progress Graph on page 141.**

Hour of Gold, Hour of Lead

Anne Morrow Lindbergh

Directions: Skim the selection, looking for main ideas and a few details. When you finish, enter your reading time and speed in the boxes below.

Reading Time

Reading Speed

Comprehension

The bare facts are that on the evening of March 1, 1932, our eighteen-month-old child, Charles Lindbergh, Jr., was taken from his crib in our home near Hopewell, New Jersey, and a note was left on the windowsill from the kidnapper demanding a ransom for his safe return. After ten weeks of negotiation and contact with the kidnapper and the handing over of the demanded ransom, the dead body of the child was found in the woods a few miles from our home. Newspapers of the time are full of accounts of the tragedy and books were written about the crime. In this period my diary reappears, and a series of letters to my mother-in-law, written almost daily after the kidnapping, give a full account of the progress of the case as we lived through it.

What needs to be explained are not outer facts but certain inner mysteries. How could I have written those letters which I have only recently recovered? I had not seen them since the day they were written. They were carefully put away among my mother-in-law's papers. When I first reread them, I was shocked and bewildered. How could I have been so self-controlled, so calm, so factual, in the midst of horror and suspense? And, above all, how could I have been so hopeful? Ten weeks of faithfully recorded details have the emotional unreality of hallucination. It was, of course, a nightmare, as my mother wrote at the time from Hopewell. "It changes but it is still a nightmare." The letters to my mother-in-law confirm the impression: "It is impossible to describe the confusion we are living in—a police station downstairs by day—detectives, police, secret service men swarming in and out— mattresses all over the dining room and other rooms at night. At any time I may be routed out of my bed so that a group of detectives may have a conference in the room. It is so terrifically unreal that I do not feel anything." Here is one key to the mystery.

Another key was hope. After the first shock, we were, to begin with, very hopeful for the safe return of the child. Everyone around us—friends, advisers, detectives, police—fed us hope, and it was this hope I tried to pass on to my mother-in-law. ("In a survey of 400 cities, 2,000 kidnapped children returned." "Never in the history of crime has there been a case of a gang bargaining over a dead person.")

Not only was I surrounded by hopeful people, I was surrounded by disciplined people. The tradition of self-control and self-discipline was strong in my own family and also in that of my husband. The people around me were courageous and I was upheld by their courage. It was also necessary to be disciplined, not only for the safety of the child I was carrying but in order to work toward the safe return of the stolen child. As in war, or catastrophe, there was a job to be done. The job and hundreds of dedicated people working with us for the same end kept us going.

Also, as in war, the case, like a great bubbling cauldron of life itself, threw up both evil and good. Greed, madness, cruelty, and indifference were countered by goodness, devotion, self-sacrifice, and courage. There were people who fluttered around the flame of publicity, politicians who came and posed for pictures next to the kidnapper's ladder. There was one city official, acting as self-appointed investigator, who woke me in the middle of the night and asked me to reenact his theory of the crime, which ended with the imaginary throwing of a baby into the furnace. And there were friends who left their homes and lives and slept on the floor of our house in order to help us. We were upheld by the devotion, loyalty, hopes, and prayers of many.

But after six weeks of unsuccessful efforts, after the ransom had been paid and no child was returned, after the clues began to run out, hope dwindled. I found it necessary, while trying to keep a surface composure for my husband, my family, and those working for and with us, to give

way somewhere to the despair banked up within me. For sanity's sake I went back to writing in my diary, two days before the body of the child was found.

A second mystery, however, both for myself and the reader, is why publish this material at all? Why expose the pain and horror of a tragedy forty years ago? Tragedy is the common lot of man. "So many people have lost children," I remind myself in the diary several weeks after our own loss. So many, I might have added, have lost husbands, wives, sweethearts, parents, whole families.

Horror, perhaps, is not as universal, and yet, looking back over the last forty years, what horrors have been experienced not only by individuals but by masses of people in the world; the holocausts of war, of civilian bombing, of concentration camps, of torture, of gas chambers, of mass executions, of Hiroshima and Nagasaki, of lynchings and civil rights murders, and "simply" of street crime that has risen in our cities to unheard-of heights. Does not this vast accumulation of horrors dwarf out of any meaning a single crime that happened long ago in a period when crime was not as frequent? Its rarity, along with the blaze of publicity that surrounded it, was one reason why it shocked the world.

The simple answer to the question is that this tragedy is such an inextricable part of my story that it cannot be left out of an honest record. Much that was written about the crime in the newspapers of the time was concocted of rumors, gossip, and fabrication. Consistent with my original premise in releasing this autobiographical material, I believe a fuller personal account of the experience should be left.

But a deeper reason moving me to publish is that suffering—no matter how multiplied—is always individual. "Pain is the most individualizing thing on earth," Edith Hamilton has written. "It is true that it is the great common bond as well, but that realization comes only when it is over. To suffer is to be alone. To watch another suffer is to know the barrier that shuts each of us away by himself. Only individuals can suffer."

Suffering is certainly individual, but at the same time it is a universal experience. There are even certain familiar stages in suffering, and familiar, if not identical, steps in coming to terms with it, as in the healing of illness—as, in fact, in coming to terms with death itself. To see these steps in another's life can be illuminating and perhaps even helpful.

What I am saying is not simply the old Puritan

truism that "suffering teaches." I do not believe that sheer suffering teaches. If suffering alone taught, all the world would be wise, since everyone suffers. To suffering must be added mourning, understanding, patience, love, openness, and the willingness to remain vulnerable. All these and other factors combined, if the circumstances are right, *can* teach and *can* lead to rebirth.

But there is no simple formula, or swift way out, no comfort, or easy acceptance of suffering. "There is no question," as Katherine Mansfield wrote, "of getting beyond it"—"The little boat enters the dark fearful gulf and our only cry is to escape—'put me on land again.' But it's useless. Nobody listens. The shadowy figure rows on. One ought to sit still and uncover one's eyes."

Contrary to the general assumption, the first days of grief are not the worst. The immediate reaction is usually shock and numbing disbelief. One has undergone an amputation. After shock comes acute early grief which is a kind of "condensed presence"—almost a form of possession. One still feels the lost limb down to the nerve endings. It is as if the intensity of grief fused the distance between you and the dead. Or perhaps, in reality, part of one dies. Like Orpheus, one tries to follow the dead on the beginning of their journey. But one cannot, like Orpheus, go all the way, and after a long journey one comes back. If one is lucky, one is reborn. Some people die and are reborn many times in their lives. For others the ground is too barren and the time too short for rebirth. Part of the process is the growth of a new relationship with the dead, that *"veritable ami mort"* Saint-Exupery speaks of. Like all gestation, it is a slow dark wordless process. While it is taking place one is painfully vulnerable. One must guard and protect the new life growing within—like a child.

One must grieve, and one must go through periods of numbness that are harder to bear than grief. One must refuse the easy escapes offered by habit and human tradition. The first and most common offerings of family and friends are always distractions ("Take her out"— "Get her away"— "Change the scene"— "Bring in people to cheer her up"—"Don't let her sit and mourn" [when it is mourning one needs]). On the other hand, there is the temptation to self-pity or glorification of grief. "I will instruct my sorrows to be proud," Constance cries in a magnificent speech in Shakespeare's *King John*. Despite her words, there is no aristocracy of grief. Grief is a great leveler. There is no highroad out.

Courage is a first step, but simply to bear the blow bravely is not enough. Stoicism is courageous, but is only a halfway house on the long road. It is a shield, permissible for a short time only. In the end one has to discard shields and remain open and vulnerable. Otherwise, scar tissue will seal off the wound and no growth will follow. To grow, to be reborn, one must remain vulnerable—open to love but also hideously open to the possibility of more suffering.

Remorse is another dead end, a kind of fake action, the only kind that seems possible at the moment. It is beating oneself in a vain attempt to make what *has* happened "*un*happen." ("If only I had done thus and so, it might not have been.") Remorse is fooling yourself, feeding on an illusion; just as living on memories, clinging to relics and photographs, is an illusion. Like the food offered one in dreams, it will not nourish; no growth or rebirth will come from it.

The inexorably difficult thing in life, and particularly in sorrow, is to face the truth. As Laurens Van der Post has written: "One of the most pathetic things about us human beings is our touching belief that there are times when the truth is not good enough for us; that it can and must be improved upon. We have to be utterly broken before we can realize that it is impossible to better the truth. It is the truth that we deny which so tenderly and forgivingly picks up the fragments and puts them together again."

Undoubtedly, the long road of suffering, insight, healing, or rebirth, is best illustrated in the Christian religion by the suffering, death, and resurrection of Christ. It is also illustrated by the story of Buddha's answer to a mother who had lost her child. According to the legend, he said that to be healed she needed only a mustard seed from a household that had never known sorrow. The woman journeyed from home to home over the world but never found a family ignorant of grief. Instead, in the paradoxical manner of myths and oracles, she found truth, understanding, compassion, and eventually, one feels sure, rebirth.

But when all is said about the universality of tragedy and the long way out, what can be added to human knowledge or insight by another example? I can only say that I could not bear to expose this story if I did not believe that one is helped by learning how other people come through their trials. Certainly I was strengthened by the personal experience of others. It is even helpful to learn the mistakes made. As the reader will see, I am familiar with the false roads:

stoicism, pride, remorse, self-pity, clinging to scraps of memories. I have not named them all; they are legion. I tried most of them. The fact that, in our case, horror was added to suffering does not change its fundamental character. The overlay of crime, horror, or accident on loss *does* increase suffering, but chiefly, I have come to feel, because it delays healing. It separates one from "the long way out," the normal process of mourning, of facing reality, of remaining open, and of eventual rebirth.

My own recovery, I realize, was greatly furthered by the love, understanding, and support of those around me. But I was also indebted to many unknown friends who had gone before me and left their testimony to illumine the shadowy path. In return I leave my own record, bearing witness to my journey, for others who may follow.

Find out your reading time and enter it in the first box on page 52. Next, turn to page 140 and look up your reading speed (words per minute). Write it in the second box. Then answer the comprehension questions.

Answer these questions without looking back at the selection. Put an *x* in the box beside the best answer for each question. Try to get 6 correct answers.

1. The ransom for the Lindbergh baby was
   - ☐ a. paid before the body was found.
   - ☐ b. not paid before the body was found.
   - ☐ c. being paid when the body was found.

2. How does Anne Lindbergh explain the optimism reflected in her letters?
   - ☐ a. She hadn't really believed her baby had been kidnapped.
   - ☐ b. She credited hope and inner discipline.
   - ☐ c. She was a naturally optimistic person.

3. What was the author's underlying purpose for publishing her account of the tragedy after so many years?
   - ☐ a. Since no account of the tragedy was presently available, she wanted to reveal the facts of the case.
   - ☐ b. She believed that writing this book would help her to accept the death of her child.
   - ☐ c. She felt that revealing the stages of her own suffering might help others in their time of suffering.

4. According to the author, we can learn from suffering only if
   - ☐ a. it is someone else's suffering.
   - ☐ b. our suffering is lengthy and intense.
   - ☐ c. we add mourning, understanding, and openness.

5. According to this selection, the first days of grief are
   - ☐ a. characterized by shock, numbness, and disbelief.
   - ☐ b. always the worst to endure.
   - ☐ c. often the most vivid memories one has of the tragedy.

6. How should the one who is grieving react when friends try to distract him or her during the early stages of grief?
   - ☐ a. Let oneself be distracted.
   - ☐ b. Refuse the escape from necessary mourning.
   - ☐ c. Pretend to be strong and unemotional.

7. How does the author feel about stoicism as a response to grief?
   - ☐ a. It can be used, but only temporarily.
   - ☐ b. It is the best way to handle grief.
   - ☐ c. It has no place in grieving.

8. According to the passage, the truly difficult thing in sorrow is to
   - ☐ a. keep from blaming others.
   - ☐ b. forget the tragedy.
   - ☐ c. face the truth.

9. The author included the Buddhist parable because it showed
   - ☐ a. that one cannot escape suffering.
   - ☐ b. how hard it is to face the truth.
   - ☐ c. that suffering is universal.

10. According to the passage, the addition of horror to loss increases suffering
    - ☐ a. mainly because it instills fear.
    - ☐ b. chiefly because it delays healing.
    - ☐ c. usually because it causes guilt.

Now correct your answers using the Answer Key on page 136. Count the number of correct answers and enter it in the last box on page 52. After you have filled in all three boxes, transfer your reading speed (words per minute) and comprehension score to the Progress Graph on page 141.

Centennial

James A. Michener

Directions: Skim the selection, looking for main ideas and a few details. When you finish, enter your reading time and speed in the boxes below.

The arrival of the horse among Our People changed many things. To take one example, it was now more pleasant to be a woman, for when the tribe moved she no longer had to haul the travois that were too heavy for the dogs. For another, the whole system of wealth was altered, and a man did not have to wait years to accumulate enough bison robes to procure the things he wanted; a horse was not only more acceptable as exchange but also more easily delivered when a transaction was agreed upon.

Hunting the bison changed, too. Three men could search out the herd, covering immense distances, and when they found it, the whole tribe did not have to trudge in pursuit; sixteen swift-riding hunters could trail it and with arrows shoot off the animals needed, then truss up the good parts and haul them back by travois.

The change was greatest for the dogs. They no longer had to haul huge loads on small travois. One horse could haul ten times as much on a big one, and dogs could be kept as pets until the time came for eating them.

Our People, in bringing the horse to Rattlesnake Buttes, unwittingly returned it to the point of its genesis, and there it flourished. A gentler tribe than their neighbors, Our People had an innate appreciation of the horse, attending more carefully to its feeding and care. The saddles Our People devised were an improvement over the heavy affairs used by the Pawnee or the crude wooden efforts of the

Reading Time

Reading Speed

Comprehension

Ute. The bridles were simpler, too, with a decoration more restrained and utilitarian. Our People adopted the horse as a member of their family, and it proved a most useful friend, for it permitted them to conquer the plains, which they had already occupied but not really explored.

On no Indian did the horse exert a more profound influence than on Lame Beaver. In 1769, when he was twenty-two, one of his fathers approached him again about marrying Blue Leaf but found him far more concerned about a horse than a wife. After the raid on the Comanche camp, the captured horses were allotted according to a sensible plan: the best-trained mounts went to the older chiefs, who needed them for ceremonial purposes; the acceptable ones went to the middle chiefs, who did the scouting for bison; and the unbroken horses went to the young warriors, who had the time to train them.

Despite the fact that Lame Beaver had masterminded the raid, he was given a nervous, unbroken pinto mare, and when he first tried to ride her she tossed him viciously into the middle of a prairiedog town. The little animals peeked out of their holes in chattering wonder as he limped after the pinto, failing to catch her on his first tries.

Again and again he sweated with the stubborn pony, not much bigger than he was, and repeatedly she pitched him over her head. Others volunteered to show him how to master her, and they went flying, too. Finally an old man said, "I heard once that the Comanche do it by taking their horses into the river."

This was such a novel idea that Lame Beaver could not at first grasp its significance, but after his pinto had resisted all other efforts, he and his friends tied her and dragged her by main strength down to the Platte. She shied away from the water, but they plunged in, keeping hold of the thongs, got a good footing, and pulled and jerked until it looked as if her neck might come off before her stubborn feet touched water. Finally, with a mighty jerk, they got her off the bank and into the stream.

She was very frightened, but they kept tugging at her until her beautiful white-and-black-and-brown body was mostly submerged. Then Lame Beaver swam close to her, so that his face was almost touching hers. He began to talk with her, slowly and with a reassuring tone: "For years and years you and I will be friends. We will ride after the bison together. You will know the feel of my knees on your flanks and turn as I bid you. We shall be friends for all the years and I will see that you get grass."

When he had spoken with her thus, and quieted somewhat the fear in her eyes, he took off the thongs and left her in the middle of the river. Without looking at her further, he swam to the bank and climbed out. She watched him go, made a halfhearted start for the opposite bank, then followed him, but when she was again safe on land she refused to let him approach.

Daily for two weeks Lame Beaver dragged his pinto into the river, and on the fifteenth day, there in the water, she allowed him to mount her, and when she felt the security of his strong legs about her, she responded and finally ran boldly onto the land and off toward the Rattlesnake Buttes.

From that moment she was his companion, and she liked nothing more than to chase after bison. Since he required both hands to manipulate his bow, she learned to respond to his knee movements, and they formed a team. She was so surefooted that he did not try to guide her, satisfied that she would find the best course, whatever the terrain. And sometimes, when he saw her running free with a group of other horses, he would catch sight of her straight back and its white patches and he would experience an emotion that could only be called love.

He was therefore disturbed when his father came to him and said, "The brother of Blue Leaf is willing that you should marry his sister, but he demands that you fulfill your promise and give him your horse."

Lame Beaver snapped, "He has his horse . . ."

"True, but he argues that that horse was given him by the council, not by you. For Blue Leaf, he demands your horse."

This outrageous request Lame Beaver refused. He still wanted Blue Leaf; certainly he had seen no other girl so attractive, but not at the price of his horse. Obstinately he declined even to discuss the matter.

But now the council intervened: "Lame Beaver promised to give a horse for Blue Leaf. Many heard how he made that vow. He cannot now change his mind and refuse to deliver the horse. It belongs to the brother of Blue Leaf."

When Lame Beaver heard this decision he was enraged, and might have done something unwise had not Red Nose come to him to speak in low, judicious tones: "There seems no escape, old friend."

"I won't surrender that pinto."

"There will be other horses."

"None like mine."

"She is no longer yours, dear friend. Tonight they will take her away."

Such a verdict seemed so unjust that Lame Beaver went before the council and cried, "I will not give up my horse. Her brother doesn't even care for the one you gave him."

"It is proper," said the elderly chief, "that men should marry in an orderly way, and we have always given presents to the brothers of our brides. A horse is a suitable gift on such an occasion. Yours must be surrendered to the brother of Blue Leaf."

On hearing this final judgment, Lame Beaver sped from the council tipi, leaped upon the pinto and dashed from the village, heading southward toward the river. He was followed by Cottonwood Knee, riding a brown pony, and as Lame Beaver was about to spur his pinto into the river, his pursuer caught up with him.

"Come back!" Cottonwood Knee called in the voice of friendship. "You and I can catch many more horses."

"Never like this one," Lame Beaver said bitterly, but in the end he dismounted and allowed Cottonwood Knee to lead the pinto back to its new owner. As Lame Beaver stood by the river, watching his horse disappear, a feeling of inconsolable grief came over him, and for five days he wandered alone. In the end he returned to camp, and Cottonwood Knee and Red Nose took him before the council, and they said, "We have ordered Blue Leaf's brother to give her to you. She is now your wife." There was a hush, then Blue Leaf's brother appeared, leading his beautiful shy sister. She stood awkwardly before the chiefs, then saw Lame Beaver standing between his friends. Slowly she came to him, extending her hands and offering herself to him. Few young husbands had ever accepted with such turbulent emotions so lovely a wife.

Lame Beaver now entered a strange world, that of the married man, in which each item of behavior was strictly defined. He could not, for example, ever speak to his wife's mother; that was totally forbidden until such time as he had presented her with some significant present. In moon periods his wife had to live in a special hut along with other women so afflicted, and while residing there, she might not speak to any man or child, lest she bring curses upon them. The consoling compensation was that with marriage he entered upon the warm and infinitely extended companionship of the Indian village, in which a man had three or four fathers and an equal number of mothers, in which all children belonged to all, and where the raising and education of the young was a common responsibility and punishment and harsh words were unknown.

It was a community in which each member did pretty much as he chose and where men who were called chiefs held that office not by heredity but by consent of their neighbors. There was no king, neither in this village nor in the tribe as a whole, only the council of older men, to which any well-comported brave might be elected by acclamation. It was one of the freest societies ever devised, hemmed in only by belief in Man-Above, reliance on Flat-Pipe, and the inherited customs of Our People. It was communal without the restraints of communism and extremely libertarian without the excesses of libertinism. It was a way of life ideally fitted to the nomads of the plains, where space was endless and the supply of bison inexhaustible.

It was galling to Lame Beaver to realize that at the next bison hunt he would have to accompany the butcher women on foot, since he had no horse, and he watched with seething anger as lesser huntsmen like his brother-in-law saddled their beasts for the chase. Blue Leaf, observing this, consoled him: "When the hunt is over you'll get two or three trusted companions and go into the Ute country and capture horses from them. If you did this against the Comanche, you can do it against the Ute."

"They keep their horses in mountains," he snapped, "and I've never been in mountains."

"I will go to reason with my brother . . . offer him a different horse . . . later, when you make other coups," and she moved toward the door of their tipi.

Lame Beaver was about to reply when all logic was driven from his mind by a brilliant flash of light. Blue Leaf could not see it, for it came from within his heart, an illumination so transcendent that it would guide him for the rest of his life.

"No," he cried in exaltation. "No more brothers. No more council. Rudely he pushed her away from the door, announcing with fierce dedication, "We shall have other horses . . . after the Sun Dance . . . many horses."

Find out your reading time and enter it in the first box on page 57. Next, turn to page 140 and look up your reading speed (words per minute). Write it in the second box. Then answer the comprehension questions.

Answer these questions without looking back at the
selection. Put an x in the box beside the best answer for
each question. Try to get 6 correct answers.

1. You can tell from the story that the term
"Our People" refers to
☐ a. the white man.
☐ b. the Pawnee.
☐ c. Lame Beaver's tribe.

2. In what way did the arrival of the horse
improve the lives of Indian women?
☐ a. They could now earn horses for
their families.
☐ b. They no longer had to haul the
heaviest travois.
☐ c. They could now ride on hunting trips.

3. The system of wealth used by Our People
before the introduction of the horse was based
on the number of
☐ a. bison robes owned by an Indian man.
☐ b. dogs owned by an Indian man.
☐ c. wives which an Indian man had.

4. As a result of the acquisition of the horse by
Our People,
☐ a. the tribe's wealth increased significantly.
☐ b. horsemeat became an important staple in
the tribe's diet.
☐ c. more efficient methods of bison hunting
could be employed.

5. How did Lame Beaver finally subdue his
unbroken mare?
☐ a. He dragged her into the river daily for
about two weeks.
☐ b. He dragged her into the river once.
☐ c. He cut down her food supply until she
was too weak to resist.

6. Lame Beaver was reluctant to marry
Blue Leaf because he
☐ a. didn't want to part with his horse.
☐ b. found Blue Leaf unattractive.
☐ c. disliked Blue Leaf's brother.

7. One unusual restriction applying to a
married man of the tribe was that he
was forbidden to speak to his wife's mother
until he
☐ a. had been married six months.
☐ b. and his wife had a child.
☐ c. gave his mother-in-law a
special gift.

8. According to the selection, each man in the
Indian village had several
☐ a. wives.
☐ b. "mothers" and "fathers."
☐ c. "brothers" and "sisters."

9. The political structure of the community
of Our People was
☐ a. a dictatorship.
☐ b. a monarchy run by a benevolent
and kind chief.
☐ c. an extremely free society with an
elected leadership.

10. You can infer from this selection that the
women of this Indian tribe
☐ a. had a subordinate role in
village life.
☐ b. were considered the equals of
the men.
☐ c. were the dominant force in village life.

Now correct your answers using the Answer Key
on page 136. Count the number of correct answers
and enter it in the last box on page 57. After you
have filled in all three boxes, transfer your reading speed (words per minute) and comprehension
score to the Progress Graph on page 141.

Body Language

Julius Fast

Directions: Skim the selection, looking for main ideas and a few details. When you finish, enter your reading time and speed in the boxes below.

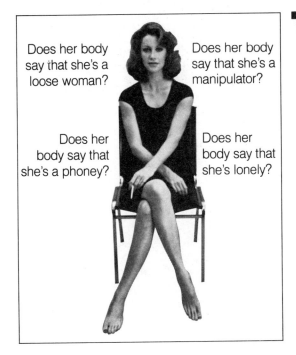

Does her body say that she's a loose woman?

Does her body say that she's a manipulator?

Does her body say that she's a phoney?

Does her body say that she's lonely?

Reading Time

Reading Speed

Comprehension

The Stare that Dehumanizes

The cowpuncher sat on his horse loosely and his fingers hovered above his gun while his eyes, ice cold, sent chills down the rustler's back.

A familiar situation? It happens in every Western novel, just as in every love story the heroine's eyes *melt* while the hero's eyes *burn* into hers. In literature, even the best literature, eyes are *steely, knowing, mocking, piercing, glowing,* and so on.

Are they really? Are they ever? Is there such a thing as a burning glance or a cold glance or a hurt glance? In truth there isn't. Far from being windows of the soul, the eyes are physiological dead ends, simply organs of sight and no more, differently colored in different people to be sure, but never really capable of expressing emotion in themselves.

And yet again and again we read and hear and even tell of the eyes being wise, knowing, good, bad, indifferent. Why is there such confusion? Can so many people be wrong? If the eyes do not show emotion, then why the vast literature, the stories and legends about them?

Of all parts of the human body that are used to transmit information, the eyes are the most important and can transmit the most subtle nuances. Does this contradict the fact that the eyes do not show emotion? Not really. While the eyeball itself shows nothing, the emotional impact of the eyes occurs because of their use and the use of the face around them. The reason they have so confounded observers is that by length of glance, by opening of eyelids, by squinting and by a dozen little manipulations of the skin and eyes, almost any meaning can be sent out.

But the most important technique of eye management is the look, or the stare. With it we can often make or break another person. How? By giving him human or nonhuman status.

Simply, eye management in our society boils down to two facts. One, we do not stare at another human being. Two, staring is reserved for a nonperson. We stare at art, at sculpture, at scenery. We go to the zoo and stare at the animals, the lions, the monkeys, the gorillas. We stare at them for as long as we please, as intimately as we please, but we do not stare at humans if we want to accord them human treatment.

We may use the same stare for the sideshow freak, but we do not really consider him a human being. He is an object at which we have paid money to stare, and in the same way we may stare at an actor on the stage. The real man is masked too deeply behind his role for our stare to bother either him or us. However, the new theater that brings the actor down into the audience often gives us an uncomfortable feeling. By virtue of involving us, the audience, the actor suddenly loses his nonperson status and staring at him becomes embarrassing to us.

If we wish pointedly to ignore someone, to treat him with an element of contempt, we can give him the same stare, the slightly unfocused look that does not really see him, the cutting stare of the socially elite.

Servants are often treated this way as are waiters, waitresses, and children. However, this may be a mutually protective device. It allows the servants to function efficiently in their overlapping universe without too much interference from us, and it allows us to function comfortably without acknowledging the servant as a fellow human. The same is true of children and waiters. It would be an uncomfortable world if each time we were served by a waiter we had to introduce ourselves and indulge in social amenities.

A Time for Looking

With unfamiliar human beings, when we acknowledge their humanness, we must avoid staring at them, and yet we must also avoid ignoring them. To make them into people rather than objects, we use a deliberate and polite inattention. We look at them long enough to make it quite clear that we see them, and then we immediately look away. We are saying, in body language, "I know you are there," and a moment later we add, "But I would not dream of intruding on your privacy."

The important thing in such an exchange is that we do not catch the eye of the one whom we are recognizing as a person. We look at him without locking glances, and then we immediately look away. Recognition is not permitted.

There are different formulas for the exchange of glances depending on where the meeting takes place. If you pass someone in the street, you may eye the oncoming person until you are about eight feet apart, then you must look away as you pass. Before the eight-foot distance is reached, each will signal in which direction he will pass. This is done with a brief look in that direction. Each will veer slightly, and the passing is done smoothly.

For this passing encounter Dr. Erving Goffman in *Behavior in Public Places* says that the quick look and the lowering of the eyes is body language for, "I trust you. I am not afraid of you."

To strengthen this signal, you look directly at the other's face before looking away.

Sometimes the rules are hard to follow, particularly if one of the two people wears dark glasses. It becomes impossible to discover just what they are doing. Are they looking at you too long, too intently? Are they looking at you at all? The person wearing the glasses feels protected and assumes that he can stare without being noticed in his staring. However, this is a self-deception. To the other person, dark glasses seem to indicate that the wearer is always staring at him.

We often use this look-away technique when we meet famous people. We want to assure them that we are respecting their privacy, that we would not dream of staring at them. The same is true of the crippled or physically handicapped. We look briefly and then look away before the stare can be said to be a stare. It is the technique we use for any unusual situation where too long a stare would be embarrassing. When we see an interracial couple, we use this technique. We might use it when we see a man with an unusual beard, with extra long hair, with outlandish clothes, or a girl with a minimal miniskirt may attract this look-and-away.

Of course, the opposite is also true. If we wish to put a person down, we may do so by staring longer than is acceptably polite. Instead of dropping our gazes when we lock glances, we continue to stare. The person who disapproves of interracial marriage or dating will stare rudely at the interracial couple. If he dislikes long hair, short dresses, or beards, he may show it with a longer-than-acceptable stare.

The Awkward Eyes

The look-and-away stare is reminiscent of the problem we face in adolescence in terms of our hands. What do we do with them? Where do we hold them? Amateur actors are also made conscious of this. They are suddenly aware of their hands as awkward appendages that must somehow be used gracefully and naturally.

In the same way, in certain circumstances, we become aware of our glances as awkward appendages. Where shall we look? What shall we do with our eyes?

Two strangers seated across from each other in a railway dining car have the option of introducing themselves and facing a meal of inconsequential and perhaps boring talk, or ignoring each other and desperately trying to avoid each other's glance. Cornelia Otis Skinner, describing such a situation in an essay, wrote, "They reread the menu, they fool with the cutlery, they inspect their own fingernails as if seeing them for the first time. Comes the inevitable moment when glances meet, but they meet only to shoot instantly away and out the window for an intent view of the passing scene."

This same awkward eye dictates our looking behavior in elevators and crowded buses and subway trains. When we get on an elevator or train with a crowd we look briefly and then look away at once without locking glances. We say, with our look, "I see you. I do not know you, but you are a human and I will not stare at you."

In the subway or bus where long rides in very close circumstances are a necessity, we may be hard put to find some way of not staring. We sneak glances, but look away before our eyes can lock. Or we look with an unfocused glance that misses the eyes and settles on the head, the mouth, the body—for any place but the eyes is an acceptable looking spot for the unfocused glance.

If our eyes do meet, we can sometimes mitigate the message with a brief smile. The smile must not be too long or too obvious. It must say, "I am sorry we have looked, but we both know it was an accident."

Bedroom Eyes

The awkward eye is a common enough occurrence for all of us to have experienced it at one time or another. Almost all actions and interractions between humans depend on mutual glances. The late Spanish philosopher Jose Ortega y Gasset, in his book *Man and People,* spoke of "the look" as something that comes directly from within a man "with the straight-line accuracy of a bullet." He felt that the eye, with its lids and sockets, its iris and pupil, was equivalent to a "whole theater with its stage and actors."

The eye muscles, Ortega said, are marvelously subtle, and because of this every glance is minutely differentiated from every other glance. There are so many different looks that it is nearly impossible to name them, but he cited, "the look that lasts but an instant and the insistent look; the look that slips over the surface of the thing looked at and the other that grips it like a hook; the direct look and the oblique look whose extreme form has its own name, 'looking out of the corner of one's eye.' "

He also listed the "sideways glance" which differs from any other oblique look although its axis is still on the bias.

Every look, Ortega said, tells us what goes on inside the person who gives it, and the intent to communicate with a look is more genuinely revealing when the sender of the look is unaware of just how he sends it.

Like other researchers into body language, Ortega warned that a look in itself does not give the entire story, even though it has a meaning. A word in a sentence has a meaning too, but only in the context of the sentence can we learn the complete meaning of the word. So too with a look. Only in the context of an entire situation is a look entirely meaningful.

There are also looks that want to see but not be seen. These the Spanish philosopher called sideways glances. In any situation we may study someone and look as long as we wish, providing the other person is not aware that we are looking, providing our look is hidden. The moment his eyes move to lock with ours, our glance must slide away. The more skilled the person, the better he is at stealing these sideways glances.

In a charming description Ortega labels one look "the most effective, the most suggestive, the most delicious and enchanting." He called it the most complicated because it is not only furtive, but it is also the very opposite of furtive because it makes it obvious that it is looking. This is the look given with lidded eyes, the sleepy look or calculating look or appraising look, the look a painter gives his canvas as he steps back from it, what the French call *les yeux en coulisse.*

Describing this look, Ortega said the lids are almost three-quarters closed and it appears to be hiding itself, but in fact the lids compress the look and "shoot it out like an arrow."

"It is the look of eyes that are, as it were, asleep but which behind the cloud of sweet drowsiness are utterly awake. Anyone who has such a look possesses a treasure."

Find out your reading time and enter it in the first box on page 61. Next, turn to page 140 and look up your reading speed (words per minute). Write it in the second box. Then answer the comprehension questions.

COMPREHENSION

Answer these questions without looking back at the selection. Put an *x* in the box beside the best answer for each question. Try to get 6 correct answers.

1. According to the selection, the eyes can transmit such subtle nuances because
   □ a. they are physiological dead ends.
   □ b. they are organs of sight.
   □ c. of their use and the use of the face around them.

2. Why is the stare the most important technique of eye management?
   □ a. The stare is used to convey great emotion.
   □ b. The stare is used to confer human or nonhuman status.
   □ c. We can stare only at persons who are our social equals.

3. According to the article, the cutting stare of the socially elite used to show contempt involves
   □ a. refusing to look at the person at all.
   □ b. using a slightly unfocused look which doesn't really see the person.
   □ c. staring closely at the person in order to cause embarrassment.

4. How do we demonstrate to passersby that they have a "human status?"
   □ a. We look at them briefly, then look away.
   □ b. We do not look at them at all.
   □ c. We lock glances as we pass each other.

5. According to the author, at what distance must we look away from an oncoming stranger on the street?
   □ a. 5 feet
   □ b. 8 feet
   □ c. 12 feet

6. From your reading of the article, in which situation would you use the "look-and-away" technique?
   □ a. You are watching a play, and your seats are very close to the stage.
   □ b. You see a person on the street whose behavior you dislike, and you want to show your disapproval.
   □ c. You pass a disabled person on the street, and you do not want to embarrass that person.

7. The "awkward eye" can be defined as
   □ a. a malfunction of the eye muscles.
   □ b. a look which we give to make the recipient feel awkward.
   □ c. the sudden feeling that we don't know what to do with our eyes.

8. To soften the effect of an accidental meeting of the eyes, we
   □ a. give a brief, impersonal smile.
   □ b. apologize profusely.
   □ c. "stare the other person down."

9. According to Ortega, the most complicated and suggestive look is the
   □ a. sideways glance.
   □ b. insistent look.
   □ c. look given with lidded eyes.

10. Which statement best summarizes the author's viewpoint about the ways we use our eyes in social situations?
   □ a. Everyone uses his eyes differently.
   □ b. The eyes are more useful than words in expressing contempt and disapproval.
   □ c. In social situations, there are predictable patterns of eye behavior.

Now correct your answers using the Answer Key on page 136. Count the number of correct answers and enter it in the last box on page 61. After you have filled in all three boxes, transfer your reading speed (words per minute) and comprehension score to the Progress Graph on page 141.

Part 2: Scanning

How to Scan

Good readers are flexible readers; they are not limited to only one type of reading. They are able to read at various speeds and at appropriate levels of comprehension. In the previous section we discussed such reading techniques as study reading, average reading, and skimming. You know that skimming is a reading technique which enables you to grasp main ideas and a few details from certain types of reading material at a high rate of speed. It is useful when you wish to discover the general idea of a selection in as little time as possible. In this section we will discuss *scanning*, another reading technique which, like skimming, enables you to obtain information in a hurry, but unlike skimming, is used only to locate specific facts.

Know Your Purpose for Reading

For any type of reading, you must begin by knowing your purpose. You must know what kind of information you are looking for and how much detail you will need. Your purpose for reading will determine the reading technique you use and the reading speed and level of comprehension you will want to maintain.

If your purpose in reading is to have a general understanding of the material in as little time as possible, it is likely that you will skim. On the other hand, if you wish only to locate a specific fact or some specific information and do not need to become familiar with all the information available, you will want to scan.

What Scanning Is

Scanning is a reading technique used when one wishes to locate a single fact or a specific bit of information without reading everything. Scanning is not new to you; you have used this reading skill many times already in your daily activities. You have used your scanning abilities when looking for the time and channel of your favorite show in the television listings of your newspaper or in television magazines. You have probably scanned pages in your telephone directory many times to find a friend's address or telephone number. When trying to locate a name in a directory, you do not read every name and number on the page; it is not necessary. You simply move your eyes quickly down the page until you locate the name, address, and number and then look no further. Scanning for information in this way should be both fast and accurate.

Steps for Scanning

Note the Arrangement of Information. Unlike skimming in which you usually know little or nothing about the material beforehand, scanning is often done with material that you do know something about. In the case of a telephone directory, for example, you already know the name of the person. You also know that the directory is arranged alphabetically according to last names. Thus, if you wish to locate the number of Joseph Sanford, you know that it will be found alphabetically with names that begin with *S*. Using the guide words at the top of the page, you can locate the correct page quickly and begin immediately to scan the alphabetical arrangement of names.

1. Alphabetical Arrangements. Much of the resource material that you will want to scan will be arranged alphabetically. A dictionary, the index of a book, a zip code directory, as well as numerous guides and reference listings, are all arranged alphabetically for quick understanding and easy location of information.

2. Nonalphabetical Arrangements. Not all material is arranged alphabetically, however. Television listings, for example, are listed by day and time. Historical data and tables may be arranged by month and year. The sports pages of your newspaper list scores by category: baseball, football, tennis, and so on. A listing of the 40 most popular songs is often arranged numerically according to the number of copies sold.

Whatever the source of reference you are using, you can be sure it is arranged in some logical way. In order to save reading time, it is important for you to know the arrangement of the material in the resource you are using. To prepare for scanning, therefore, you must take a few minutes to discover the organization of the material. Once you understand the arrangement of information, you can proceed immediately to find the section or page most likely to contain the information you want.

3. Prose Material. There is a third type of material which you may have occasion to scan. In order to answer a specific question or to locate a specific bit of information, you may want to scan an article in a newspaper or magazine, or a section of an encyclopedia or similar source of reference. It may not be necessary to read the entire article to find the particular information you need. Instead, you will want to save time by scanning to locate the part of the article that will be useful to you. In order to scan quickly and efficiently, you must become familiar with the arrangement of the material. Take a few minutes to read the title and subheads, look at the illustrations, and read the first and last paragraphs. This will give you a general idea of the order of ideas and topics. Once you understand the arrangement of thoughts in the selection, you will have a better idea where the information you want may be located, and you can quickly turn to that section of the material. In this way you will be prepared to scan quickly and efficiently for the specific information you need.

Keep Clue Words in Mind. Once you have found the section likely to contain the information you need, you are ready to begin scanning. Have in mind some clue words or phrases associated with the specific facts you are looking for. For example, when scanning the telephone directory, your clue word would be the person's last name along with your knowledge of alphabetical order. In the case of a newspaper sports page, your clue words for locating the baseball scores would be *baseball, run,* the names of the teams, and the cities the teams represent.

Clue words are also useful when scanning magazine articles and encyclopedias. If you want to know the population of New York City, for example, you would locate the section of the encyclopedia which discusses New York City. Your clue words when scanning this section would be *population, census, inhabitants,* and, of course, any numbers.

Speed

The purpose in scanning is to locate information quickly. Thus, a high rate of speed is essential. Once you find the appropriate section of the material and have clue words in mind, you should strive to scan as much of the printed matter as you can in the least amount of time. Remember that you are searching for specific words; don't allow yourself to become distracted by words or ideas unrelated to the information you are scanning to find.

If you find yourself beginning to read sentences or paragraphs, stop reading and begin again to move your eyes in a scanning pattern. Once you have located the clue words, start to read more carefully to find the specific information you need.

Accuracy

Accuracy is just as essential as speed when scanning. Since you are looking for specific information, it is important that it be accurate. If you scan to discover the number of the train leaving for New York City, you will be dismayed later to find yourself on the train to Washington, D.C., because your scanning procedure resulted in inaccurate information. Once you have scanned to find the information you need, take the time to read it carefully. Your goal should be 100 percent accuracy.

Advantages of Scanning

Scanning is a reading technique that you will use frequently. You scan a dictionary for a particular word, a telephone directory for a friend's number, and the newspaper headlines for an article that you want to read. You scan best-seller lists, television sections, department store directories, and bus schedules.

As a student, you will find scanning to be a valuable skill for locating information in dictionaries, indexes, encyclopedias, almanacs, and other reference materials. Scanning is also a fast and efficient way to locate material in your textbooks. Often you may want to refer to information you've studied early in the term to relate it to something new, to clarify a point in question, or to locate definitions or theories you'd like to review. Scanning enables you to locate the section you need quickly so that you may spend your time rereading the relevant material more carefully.

The following section will help you improve your scanning skills. Use this text to develop scanning speed and accuracy. Practice now will save you time in the future and make you a more flexible reader.

How to Use Part 2: Scanning

1. **Read the Lesson.** Learn what scanning is, when to scan, and how to scan. Reread and review if necessary.

2. **Complete the Practice Exercises.** Apply what was learned in the lesson to the exercises to build scanning skill. Follow these steps.

   a) **Scan for the Answers.** Read the introductory information and directions for each exercise. Then read each question and scan for the answer.

   b) **Record Scanning Time.** Follow the instructions for timing the exercise. Record your total time in the space provided on the question page. As an alternative to timing, teachers may use these exercises as group races by having students compete against one another for speed and accuracy.

   c) **Check Your Answers.** Correct your answers using the answer key on page 137. Record the total number correct in the space provided on each question page.

3. **Practice Daily.** Apply scanning techniques on your own, using materials you encounter every day.

Scanning Drills

Scanning Alphabetical Lists

Some materials you will want to scan are arranged alphabetically. A solid understanding of the rules of alphabetical order will enable you to scan these materials quickly.

You know that words are alphabetized by the first letter: *after, book.* Words that have the same first letter are alphabetized by the second letter: *cake, clock.* When the first *two* letters of words to be alphabetized are the same, the words are arranged according to the third letter, *cream* and *crow*, and so on. Thus, an alphabetical list of the above examples would be: *after, book, cake, clock, cream, crow.*

Knowing how to alphabetize efficiently is a basic scanning skill. The words in the following exercise have similar beginning letters and so will give you practice in alphabetical order up to the sixth letter.

Directions: Look briefly at the list of words on page 76. Notice that the words are in alphabetical order, that the first word begins with *i,* and that the last word begins with *l.*

Scan the word list to find each of the 20 words located on page 77. As you locate each word in the list, write the word which precedes it in the blank provided. Study the example first.

It is important to scan quickly and efficiently. You may want to time yourself with a stopwatch for each item. Start the watch as soon as you begin to scan the word list, and stop the watch when you have located the word. Do not time the period it takes you to record your answer.

Record your scanning time in the space provided. As you begin to scan for a new word, try to improve on your previous speed. When you have completed the exercise, find your total scanning time. Compare your total time with that of the other members of your class.

Strive for 100 percent accuracy. Scanning at a high rate of speed is useful only if you find the exact information you need. When finished, correct your answers using the answer key on page 137.▶

imminently	incautiously	indulgently	instinctively	irresistibly
immoderately	incessantly	industriously	instructively	irresolutely
immodestly	inchoately	ineffably	instrumentally	irrespectively
immorally	incisively	ineffaceably	insubordinately	irresponsibly
immortally	inclemently	ineffectively	insufferably	irreverently
immovably	inclusively	ineffectually	insufficiently	irreversibly
immutably	incoherently	inefficiently	insupportably	irrevocably
impalpably	incommensurately	inelegantly	insurmountably	irritably
impartially	incomparably	ineligibly	intangibly	jaggedly
impassably	incompatibly	ineluctably	integrally	jauntily
impassively	incompetently	ineptly	intelligently	jealously
impatiently	incomprehensibly	inequitably	intelligibly	jerkily
impeccably	inconclusively	ineradicably	intemperately	jocosely
impecuniously	incongruously	inertly	intensively	jocularly
impenetrably	inconsequently	inescapably	intently	jocundly
impenitently	inconsiderably	inevitably	interchangeably	jollily
imperatively	inconsiderately	inexactly	interestedly	jovially
imperfectly	inconsistently	inexcusably	interestingly	joyfully
imperially	inconsolably	inexorably	interiorly	joyously
imperiously	inconspicuously	inexpediently	interjectionally	jubilantly
imperishably	inconstantly	inexpensively	intermittently	judicially
impermeably	incontestably	inexplicably	interrogatively	judiciously
impertinently	incontinently	inextinguishably	intimately	juicily
imperturbably	incontrovertibly	inextricably	intolerantly	justifiably
imperviously	inconveniently	infallibly	intractably	keenly
impetuously	incorporeally	infamously	intransigently	killingly
impiously	incorrectly	infectiously	intransitively	knavishly
impishly	incorrigibly	inferentially	intrepidly	laboriously
implacably	incorruptibly	infernally	intricately	lackadaisically
impolitely	incredibly	inflammably	introspectively	laggardly
impoliticly	incredulously	inflexibly	intrusively	lamely
importantly	incuriously	influentially	intuitively	languidly
importunately	indecently	informally	inversely	languishingly
impotently	indecisively	infrequently	inveterately	languorously
impracticably	indecorously	ingeniously	invidiously	lankly
impractically	indefatigably	ingenuously	invincibly	lasciviously
impregnably	indefeasibly	ingloriously	inviolably	lastingly
impressively	indefensibly	inharmoniously	inviolately	latently
improperly	indefinably	inhospitably	invitingly	laudably
improvidently	indefinitely	inhumanely	involuntarily	laughably
imprudently	indelibly	inhumanly	invulnerably	lavishly
impudently	indelicately	inimically	irascibly	lawfully
impulsively	indescribably	iniquitously	irately	lawlessly
impurely	indestructibly	injudiciously	irefully	laxly
inaccurately	indeterminately	innately	iridescently	lazily
inactively	indicatively	innocently	irksomely	learnedly
inadequately	indigenously	innocuously	ironically	legibly
inadmissably	indigestibly	inoffensively	irrationally	legitimately
inadvertently	indignantly	inopportunely	irreclaimably	lengthily
inalienably	indirectly	inquisitively	irreconcilably	leniently
inanely	indiscernibly	insanely	irrecoverably	levelly
inanimately	indiscreetly	inscrutably	irredeemably	lewdly
inapplicably	indiscriminately	insensately	irrefragably	lexicographer
inappropriately	indisputably	inseparably	irrefutably	libellously
inaptly	indissolubly	insidiously	irregularly	libelously
inarticulately	indistinctly	insignificantly	irrelevantly	liberally
inattentively	indistinguishably	insincerely	irreligiously	licentiously
inaudibly	indivisibly	insipidly	irremediably	licitly
inauspiciously	indolently	insistently	irremovably	lifelessly
incalculably	indubitably	insolently	irreparably	light-heartedly
incapably	inductively	instantaneously	irreproachably	light-mindedly

EXAMPLE

impishly

impiously

In this example, *impishly* is preceded in the word list by *impiously.*

Time for Entire D[...]

Start

Finish

Word to Locate	**Preceding Word**	**Time for Each Word**
1. keenly	1. _____	1. _____ seconds
2. jaggedly	2. _____	2. _____ seconds
3. laboriously	3. _____	3. _____ seconds
4. learnedly	4. _____	4. _____ seconds
5. jealously	5. _____	5. _____ seconds
6. inaccurately	6. _____	6. _____ seconds
7. licentiously	7. _____	7. _____ seconds
8. incalculably	8. _____	8. _____ seconds
9. intangibly	9. _____	9. _____ seconds
10. ironically	10. _____	10. _____ seconds
11. impeccably	11. _____	11. _____ seconds
12. inconclusively	12. _____	12. _____ seconds
13. joyously	13. _____	13. _____ seconds
14. lawlessly	14. _____	14. _____ seconds
15. immorally	15. _____	15. _____ seconds
16. incongruously	16. _____	16. _____ seconds
17. inexorably	17. _____	17. _____ seconds
18. interestedly	18. _____	18. _____ seconds
19. indiscriminately	19. _____	19. _____ seconds
20. inexplicably	20. _____	20. _____ seconds

ANSWER KEY: PAGE 137

Number Correct [ ]   Scanning Time [ ]

Scanning Guide Words

Guide words are the words at the top of the page in many reference works, such as a dictionary or telephone directory. They help you locate alphabetically arranged entries. Some dictionaries do not use whole words for guide words; instead, the first three letters of the word are provided. There are always two guide words that represent the first word or entry on the page and the last word or entry on the page. If you want to find a word in a dictionary, for example, it is a very useful skill to scan through the dictionary looking just at guide words; then when you find the right page, you scan down the page to find the exact word. The following exercises will improve your skill in using guide words.

Directions: The guide words for pages 94 through 117 of one dictionary are shown on page 80. Note that the first guide word indicates that the first word on page 94 of the dictionary begins with *gen*. The second guide word for page 94 indicates that the last word on that page begins with *gla*. You know, therefore, that all the words

on page 94 come after *gen* alphabetically but before *gla*. Thus, *gh*ost would be found on page 94, but *g*arden and *g*rand would not.

Scan the guide words to discover the page on which each of the words in Part A would appear. When you have located the appropriate pair of guide words for the word you wish to look up, write the page number in the blank provided. Study the example first.

Speed is essential when scanning a dictionary to locate a word. Timing yourself may help to improve your speed. Time yourself to see how long it takes you to locate the first 15 words. Record this time in the space provided in the box at the bottom of the page. Time yourself again on numbers 16 through 30. Strive to scan this second group of 15 faster than the first. Record your time in the space provided at the bottom of the page.

Your goal should be 100 percent accuracy. Searching for the spelling or meaning of a word on the wrong page will cost you valuable study time. When finished, correct your answers using the answer key on page 137. Record your total number of correct answers. ▶

116 ins-int
114 ine-ink
112 ina-ind
110 ill-imp
108 hov-hur
106 hob-hoo
104 hel-hid
102 har-hea
100 gus-ham
98 gre-gro
96 gob-gra
94 gen-gla

int-inv 117
ink-ins 115
ind-ine 113
imp-ina 111
hur-ill 109
hoo-hov 107
hid-hob 105
hea-hel 103
ham-har 101
gro-gus 99
gra-gre 97
gla-gob 95

gen·u·flect (jen′yə·flekt) v.i. To bend the knee, as in worship. [< L genu knee + flectere to bend] —gen′u·flec′tion n.
gen·u·ine (jen′yoo·in) adj. 1. Being of the origin, authorship, or character claimed. 2. Not spurious or counterfeit. [< L genuinus innate] —gen′u·ine·ly adv. —gen′u·ine·ness n.
ge·nus (jē′nəs) n. pl. gen·e·ra (jen′ər·ə) 1. Biol. A grouping or category of plants and animals ranking next above the species and next below the family or subfamily. 2. Logic A class of things divisible into two or more subordinate classes or species. 3. A particular sort, kind, or class. [< L, race, kind]
-geny combining form Mode of production of; generation or development of: anthropogeny. [< Gk. gen-, stem of gignesthai: to become]
geo- combining form Earth; ground; soil. [< Gk. gē earth]
ge·o·cen·tric (jē′ō·sen′trik) adj. 1. Calculated or viewed relative to the earth's center. 2. Assuming that the earth is the center of the universe. Also ge′o·cen′tri·cal. —ge′o·cen′tri·cal·ly adv.
ge·o·chem·is·try (jē′ō·kem′is·trē) n. The branch of chemistry dealing with ... tion of the earth's crust. —ge′o·chem′ist ... ij. —ge′o·chem′ist ...
...de (jē′ōd) ... ular 1...

glass blowing The art of shaping glass by blowing air through a tube into a mass of molten glass.
glass·ful (glas′fool) n. pl. ·fuls The amount contained in a drinking glass.
glass·ware (glas′wâr′) n. Articles made of glass.
glass wool Fibers of spun glass of woollike appearance, used for insulation, filters, etc.
glass·works (glas′wûrks′) n.pl. (usu. construed as sing.) A factory where glass is made.
glass·y (glas′ē) adj. glass·i·er, glass·i·est 1. Resembling glass. 2. Fixed, blank, and uncomprehending: a glassy stare. —glass′i·ly adv. —glass′i·ness n.
glau·co·ma (glô·kō′mə, glou-) n. A disease of the eye characterized by ... of fluids within the eyeball ... of vision.
glaze (glāz) ... [< L < Gr ... Pat ... as a win ... gl

EXAMPLE

guilt _____99_____

In this example, the word *guilt* would be found on page 99 since alphabetically it follows *gro* and precedes *gus*.

Time for Items 1–15

Start	
Finish	

Time for Items 16–30

Start	
Finish	

Word to Look Up	Page Number	Word to Look Up	Page Number
1. hazard	1. _____	16. hysteria	16. _____
2. gorge	2. _____	17. grimace	17. _____
3. hermit	3. _____	18. inhibit	18. _____
4. hundred	4. _____	19. hedge	19. _____
5. grip	5. _____	20. guest	20. _____
6. haven	6. _____	21. intangible	21. _____
7. immune	7. _____	22. influx	22. _____
8. ginger	8. _____	23. historian	23. _____
9. incorrect	9. _____	24. gorilla	24. _____
10. gymnasium	10. _____	25. hawk	25. _____
11. homicide	11. _____	26. hit	26. _____
12. in	12. _____	27. grief	27. _____
13. glutton	13. _____	28. go	28. _____
14. hotel	14. _____	29. incomplete	29. _____
15. increase	15. _____	30. interest	30. _____

ANSWER KEY: PAGE 137

Items 1–15 ▶	Scanning Time		Items 16–30 ▶	Scanning Time	
	Number Correct			Number Correct	

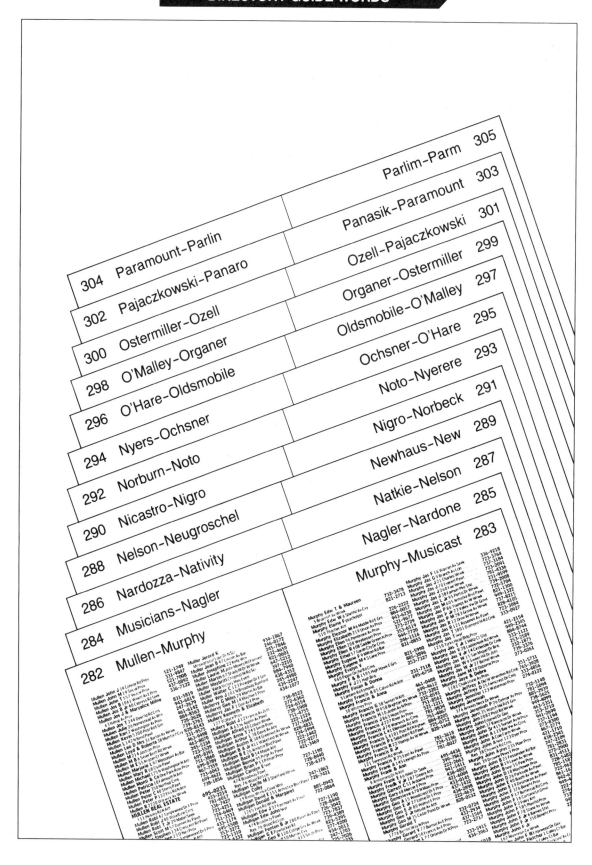

Parlim–Parm 305

Panasik–Paramount 303

304 Paramount–Parlin

Ozell–Pajaczkowski 301

302 Pajaczkowski–Panaro

Organer–Ostermiller 299

300 Ostermiller–Ozell

Oldsmobile–O'Malley 297

298 O'Malley–Organer

Ochsner–O'Hare 295

296 O'Hare–Oldsmobile

Noto–Nyerere 293

294 Nyers–Ochsner

Nigro–Norbeck 291

292 Norburn–Noto

Newhaus–New 289

290 Nicastro–Nigro

Natkie–Nelson 287

288 Nelson–Neugroschel

Nagler–Nardone 285

286 Nardozza–Nativity

Murphy–Musicast 283

284 Musicians–Nagler

282 Mullen–Murphy

The following exercise will give you additional practice scanning guide words. The guide words for pages 282–305 of one telephone directory are shown on the left.

   Look at the last name of the person you want to look up. If you are asked to look up the name of a company or institution, look at the first word in the title. The name or word you are looking for is alphabetically between one pair of guide words. Scan the guide words until you discover on which page the name would appear and write the page number on the line provided.

   See how fast you can find the page numbers for the first 10 names. Then take another timing as you try to do the second 10 faster.

Time for Items 1–10	
Start	
Finish	
Time for Items 11–20	
Start	
Finish	

EXAMPLE
Joseph Palmer   _302_

The telephone number of Joseph Palmer would be located on page 302 since *Palmer* follows *Pajaczkowski* and precedes *Panaro* alphabetically.

Name to Look Up	Page Number	Name to Look Up	Page Number
1. Jack Murray	1. _____	11. Fred Parker	11. _____
2. Peter Neff	2. _____	12. Joseph Norton	12. _____
3. Nelso Petroleum Products	3. _____	13. M. Paluskiewicz	13. _____
4. B. A. Nielsen	4. _____	14. Palisade Poultry Farm	14. _____
5. Multi Construction Co.	5. _____	15. E. T. Nolte	15. _____
6. Francis O'Brien	6. _____	16. Odyssey Travel	16. _____
7. Nova Realty	7. _____	17. Joseph Olivera	17. _____
8. Arthur Paige	8. _____	18. Patrick North	18. _____
9. S. Nadelman	9. _____	19. Old Bridge TV	19. _____
10. H. A. Olsen	10. _____	20. Harold Osborne	20. _____

ANSWER KEY: PAGE 137			
Items 1–10 ▶	Scanning Time	**Items 11–20 ▶**	Scanning Time
	Number Correct		Number Correct

Scanning Telephone Directories

Looking up numbers in a telephone directory is one of the most common uses of scanning skills. You don't read the whole page; you merely scan until you find the desired information—in this case the telephone number. Here are a couple of hints that will save you time.

Memorize the Spelling. Take a moment to see that you have correctly memorized the spelling. Looking back to check the spelling takes more time than getting it right the first time.

Memorize the Number. When you find the number, take a moment to memorize it by saying it slowly to yourself. You can easily put 7 digits into your short-term memory. Say it clearly to yourself, then turn the page and write it down. Don't give up and memorize just the first half of the number, then look back to find the second half of the number. That takes more time and can cause more errors. The space between the numbers is put there to help you—so use it. Say the first 3 digits, pause, then say the last 4 digits. Don't worry that you will forget the first 3 while you are saying the last 4; psychologists have already found that most people can easily retain the whole number and give it back in

serial fashion (from first to last). Only fear and/or lack of confidence can cause you to fumble. But you must put the entire number into your short-term memory clearly and correctly the first time.

Directions: Look briefly at the following telephone directory page. Notice that the entries are in alphabetical order according to last name.

Scan the telephone listings to locate the numbers of the people listed on page 87. Remember to memorize the spelling of the name before you scan for the corresponding number. Once you have located the number, memorize all 7 digits and write them on the blank provided. Study the example first.

Time yourself on the first 10 and record your time in the space provided after number 10. Time yourself again on numbers 11 through 20. Strive to scan this second group faster than the first. Record your second timing in the space provided after number 20.

Aim for 100 percent accuracy. When finished, correct your answers using the answer key on page 137. ▶

Hamel Geo 16SackettWrwk -------758-3592
Hamel Geo A 152WilmarthAttl ---222-9540
Hamel Geo H 11CrestVwDrSfld ----949-3963
Hamel Gerald A 179PinneryAvWrwk 738-2672
Hamel Gerald P 102BenftProv ----274-5694
Hamel H J 117HybridDrCrns ---944-8017
Hamel Henry H ShoreDrGloc ----949-0776
Hamel Howard WinthropRdEGrn ---884-5245
Hamel Irene Mrs 495BroadCF ----723-5046
Hamel Irene M 111GeslerProv -----831-3556
Hamel J Vincent Sgt
    101GaytonAvWrwk----737-0782
Hamel Janet 18SweetAvPawt ----724-4116
Hamel John W 20HodgesAttl ----222-0283
Hamel Jos 37MapleAttl -------222-7229
Hamel Jos A 16HornbneCrns ----941-8847
Hamel Jos G 55DarlngCF --------726-0620
Hamel Jos R 720PineCF --------723-1657
Hamel Lawrence A 25BeckerAvJstn 231-1768
Hamel Leo J 37SumnerAvCrns ---942-0779
Hamel Louis C 13TallmnAvEPrv --434-8452
Hamel Lucien 1360NewportAvPawt 724-7837
Hamel M E 209MarylandAvWrwk --737-1195
Hamel Margaret 151HuntCF ----724-9387
Hamel Margaret 21LincolnAvCF ---722-1657
Hamel Maurice N 38TuckerCF ---726-2786
Hamel Michael W 158TerraceAvCrns 943-5399
Hamel N 127SamuelAvPawt ------722-3554
Hamel Napoleon J 16RoseDrPawt -723-8407
Hamel Noe 11EchoCF -----------723-2672
Hamel Paul E Jr
    47BrendardAvWrwk--738-3208
Hamel Paul E Sr
    153 InmanAvWrwk--739-3138
Hamel Philip PawtucketAvBris ---253-4225
Hamel Pierre J 15EchoCF -------722-9609
Hamel Ralph K HillFarmCov ----397-9583
Hamel Real
    JenckesRdCumb--Woonsocket 767-3966
Hamel Rene CircleDrCov --------397-7323
Hamel Richard P 7LakeVwDrSfld --949-0347
Hamel Robt J 16CherryWrn ----245-5386
Hamel Robt L 17UndrwdAvWrwk -781-3811
Hamel Robt M 16HighridgeDrCmb 333-2125
Hamel Robt W 103BinghmWrwk ---737-4964
Hamel Robt S 18JenkinsProv -----751-0396
Hamel Ronald J 30TenthStProv ---274-6516
Hamel Russell G 20SweetRdSfld ---231-4307
Hamel S A 97ChandlerAvPawt ---728-8607
Hamel Stephanie A
    23ArchambaultAvWWrwk--828-8363
Hamel Steven 16CherryWrn ------247-0245
Hamel Tool Co
    115PennsylvaniaAvWrwk--737-2271
Hamel Valerie 33MonticelloRdPawt 728-7015
Hamel Wm 415SunsetAvNPrv -----353-3887
Hamel Wm A 65MainEGrn -------884-2805
Hamel Wm J 7LakeViewDrSfld ---949-1262
Hamel Wm Jos 32BalchPawt -----723-2884
Hamel Y 5CathedralSqProv ------272-9419
Hamelin Gary M 76ArmstrongProv -272-2974
HAMER—See also Hamer
Hamer Albert 20MaryPawt ------724-8035
Hamer Chas 96BialsdlAvPawt ----722-9896
Hamer Morton K 46ParisPawt ---725-5046
Hamer Oscar H 28HillTopDrCrns --463-6328
Hamer Saml 71DaggettAvPawt ---725-2166
Hames Francis M
    16BryantPlWWrwk--821-3204
Hames Francis R
    1416½MainWWrwk--821-6730
Hames Jim 260ProvdnceAvEPrv ---433-2863
Hames Martin F 190 IrvingRdWrwk 781-7296
Hames Thos 222ResrvrAvProv ----461-1960
Hames Wm J 143 IndianaAvProv --781-7657
Hametz Irwin Dr 226FourthProv --521-5699
HAMILL—See also Hamel
Hamill Cornelius A 14RillProv -----521-7075
Hamill John J 277GroveProv -----521-6467
Hamill M 1ValleyProv ----------351-6973
Hamill Rose Mrs 3AbbottPawt -----725-5234
Hamill W H T Mrs
    162RogerWmsAvEPrv--434-9151
Hamill Walter R BungyRdGloc ---647-7377
Hamill Wilfred M 908HopeBris ---253-6090
Hamill Wm J 38MadisnPawt ----725-7866
Hamlin Wm J PinecrestDrGloc ---647-2875
Hamilton A A 28ApolloRdEPrv ---434-5872
Hamilton A J Jr 81FourthEGrn ---884-4615
Hamilton A V 45ByronAvEPrv ----434-6674

Hamilton David & A L
    9BenjaminWrwk--884-2163
Hamilton David E 389ElmNAtt ---695-6516
Hamilton Donald
    33AlfredDrowneRdBar--245-5809
Hamilton Dorothy R
    204CoyleAvPawt--725-3989
Hamilton Earl D 24RumstickDrBar 245-1276
Hamilton Edwin R 36SlaterAttl ---222-3227
Hamilton Edwin R
    1879WarwckAvWrwk--737-8394
Hamilton Elmer W
    45SuburbanPkwyWrwk--737-5366
Hamilton Emma 495WestAvPawt --725-3862
Hamilton Ernest G SebilRdSfld --231-5044
Hamilton Estelle M Mrs
    26ParksdAvPawt--723-0353
Hamilton Eugene P
    571NarrgnstPkwyWrwk--467-6325
Hamilton Francis H 216EighthProv 751-1608
Hamilton Francis W
    40CollegeRdProv--861-4293
Hamilton Frank A Jr 54ArizonaCov 828-2477
Hamilton Fred 547WillettAvProv ---433-3516
Hamilton Fredk 11NewbryProv ---521-9056
Hamilton Fredk & Staff optmtrsts
    1JacksonWalkwayProv--421-8387
Hamilton Fredk W 758MainWrn --245-5660
Hamilton G M Mrs
    38 OldCountyRdBar--246-0040
Hamilton Gary 12LockwoodWrwk -828-8077
Hamilton Gordon L
    485NWashngtnNAtt--699-4876
Hamilton Hotel of Washington D C
    703 IndBankBldgProv--331-3331
Hamilton House 276AngellProv ---331-7480
Hamilton J Albert 18WParkProv --861-9368
Hamilton J Fraser textls
    86WeybossetProv--421-2906
    Res rr764NewprtAvPawt ------725-9848
Hamilton J M
    199SunnybrookDrNKng--884-5491
Hamilton Jas L Dr
    262LawnacreDrCrns--943-7434
Hamilton Jas P 72WelfareAvCrns --781-0532
Hamilton Jas V 18SunsetDrBar ---245-4320
Hamilton John V
    571NarrgnstPkwyWrwk--467-5610
Hamilton John W SCountyTrlEGrn -884-3633
Hamilton Jon R
    148HoraceDarlingDrNAtt--695-1772
Hamilton Jos 440LonsdlAvPawt --723-8323
Hamilton Jos C 25SunsetDrBar ---245-1279
Hamilton Kenneth L
    2345MiddleRdEGrn--884-9195
Hamilton Kenneth V
    458PowerRdPawt--523-6031
Hamilton Laura 100HighPlainvil -695-3110
Hamilton Leo J 100AtwlsAvProv --831-3796
Hamilton Leon C Jr
    101CumbrlndAvAttl--761-7339
Hamilton M M 85ByronBlvdWrwk -467-8431
Hamilton Mae L 100BroadProv ---331-2476
Hamilton Maurice L 16WestStAttl --222-5117
Hamilton Mildred C 1ValleyProv --861-4729
Hamilton Mills Army & Navy Store
    33WashngtnWWrwk--821-7891
Hamilton Paul D
    986LongvwDrhAttl--399-7538
Hamilton Paul H 46TownsendPawt --246-1462
Hamilton R G 43MarcyCrns ------461-1351
Hamilton Ralph N
    28BakersCreekRdWrwk--737-4840
Hamilton Ralph N Jr
    155ColeAvWrwk--737-7028
Hamilton Raymond M
    24KnowlesLcln--722-4074
Hamilton Richard 62GlenroseDrEPrv 433-1404
Hamilton Richard E DivEGrn -----884-4114
Hamilton Rick D 8TarklynAttlFls -695-5594
Hamilton Robt A
    48WoodhvnBlvdNPrv--231-1738
Hamilton Robt G 35CreightnProv -861-7057
Hamilton Robt J 229SeymourWrn --245-6467
Hamilton Robt W 14EastDrNAtt --695-5224
Hamilton Ronald R 50CoitAvWWrwk 821-6227
Hamilton Stephen K
    369NewprtAvSAttl--761-5088
Hamilton Thos A Jr
    80EBelAirRdCrns--942-1711

Hamlett Otha Earl
    MtViewAvNKgtwn--884-7436
Hamlin Ambrose 148 OxfordProv -941-7520
Hamlin Ambrose Jas Jr
    6MansfldProv--331-7207
Hamlin Arthur 30WeaverWWrwk --828-4662
Hamlin Chas 167BriggProv ------941-4289
Hamlin Dusten 41VineWWrwk ---822-0091
Hamlin Hannibal neuro surg
    270BeneftProv--331-5353
Hamlin Hannibal Mrs
    270BenefitProv--272-0018
Hamlin Richard ManningCtCov ----828-4212
Hamlin Robt H 105EManngProv --521-5131
Hamlyn Betty 100WashngtnAvProv 461-2638
Hamlyn John F 74PhebeProv -----861-5816
Hamlyn Russell S
    107WarwickAvProv--461-5363
Hamlyn Stuart F
    273NorwoodAvCrns--461-1953
Hamlyn Wm H 52StaffrdPawt ----723-1022
Hamm David 956WarrenAvEPrv --434-3759
Hamm Jas J Jr 10AcornLnWWrwk 826-0935
Hamm Jos J 8BeachwdDrCmb ---725-0696
Hamm Margaret C
    170NewMeadowRdBar--245-2786
Hamm Roger D LakeShoreDrGloc --949-3846
Hammack Rick 201AngellProv ---272-6861
Hamman Benj F
    287DiamondHillRdWrwk--738-0979
Hammar Arthur W 66RooseveltWrwk 467-7341
Hammar David B GreenvilleRdScit -647-5070
Hammar H 246MiltonRdProv ----781-2541
Hammarlund Chas N
    94CrownAvEPrv--434-3297
Hammarlund Ellery.W
    211CntryClubDrWrwk--467-9812
Hammarlund Nelson E Mrs
    3663PawtucketAvEPrv--433-4835
Hammarlund O Leroy
    695NBwayEPrv--438-4714
Hammart Inc comb wndws
    176WashngtnCF--726-0733
    952MinerlSprngAvPawt
Hammel-Dahl ITT 175PostRdWrwk 781-6200
HAMMER—See also Hamer
Hammer Bertha 41NewportAvSAttl 399-8675
Hammer Betty 41NewportAvSAttl 399-8675
Hammer C J OldRiverRdLcln -----333-1079
Hammer Eugene C 34DelwayRdCrns 941-4995
Hammer Frank J 41NewprtAvSAttl 761-7032
Hammer Philip 74ForbesEPrv ----437-1435
Hammerle Brooke 99GovernorProv 521-1215
Hammerschlag Peter 47FrenchPawt 724-2184
Hammerschmidt Angella
    48NickrsnCrns--944-6253
Hammerschmidt Angella
    3WesternHillsLnCrns--942-4161
Hammerschmidt Herbert E
    3WesternHillsLnCrns--942-4161
Hammerschmidt Kenneth E
    659PikeAvAttl--222-4970
Hammerschmidt Robt
    45 OverlkDrWrwk--884-7936
Hammerschmidt Robt I
    130AltheaProv--861-7693
Hammersmith Harris Warwick ----739-8729
Hammerton A 12CamacPawt ----725-6949
HAMMOND—See also Hayman Heyman
Heymann
Hammond Aubrey F 76CampProv --521-7624
Hammond B F 77SuffolkDrNKng ---884-0028
Hammond & Barrie Div Stillman White Co
    Inc 43RogerWmsAvEPrv--434-5170
Hammond Benj W 365BroadCmb ---724-6127
Hammond Benny F 58JerryLnNKng 885-2813
Hammond Bonnie L
    1115GreenwichAvWrwk--737-0778
Hammond Bruce W 28CemeteryProv 421-8842
Hammond Burton D
    780TollGteRdWrwk--821-5624
Hammond Charlene 145CotgePawt 726-4694
Hammond Clarence L
    35DouglsCirSfld--949-0727
Hammond D G 68RichmondCF ----725-1841
Hammond Donald E HartfordPkeFos 647-5263
Hammond Donald G
    50Studleyavvrwwk--737-8290
Hammond Donald T 18ElmNPrv --353-9684
Hammond E A 86SlaterPawt -----728-2652

Hammond Jas H 10BarryRdProv - 521-6684
Hammond Jas W 2408PawtAvEPrv 438-5387
Hammond Jas W Jr 64DyerAvEPrv 437-0897
Hammond John E 76LymanNAtt --699-2396
Hammond John E 59MarshallAvCmb 723-4545
Hammond John R
    11HawthorneAvEPrv--434-0933
Hammond John W 86ThirdProv ---421-6310
Hammond Jos 16SaundrsPawt ---723-6648
Hammond Juanita
    296PottersAvProv--941-4581
Hammond Kenneth A
    AnanWadeRdFos--647-5273
Hammond Lester H
    OldHartfrdPkFos--647-3413
Hammond M E 116BeaufrtProv ----272-4395
Hammond M E 20LarsonDrWrwk --738-9430
Hammond M E
    734MinerlSpringAvPawt--724-6663
Hammond Marilyn R Mrs
    14PaquinRdBar--245-4895
Hammond Marshall
    119AnawanRdNAtt--695-6866
Hammond Milton W
    16CrescentAvCrns 944-9047
Hammond Motor Sales
    263DexterPawt--725-3030
Hammond Norman L
    AnanWadeRdGloc--647-5843
Hammond P Great RdLcln --------724-8606
Hammond P 154TaberAvProv ----521-4843
Hammond Pamela A
    19 OldCarriageRdWWrwk--828-9260
Hammond R
    6200PostRdNKingstown--884-7899
Hammond R A 27BowmanDrWrwk -738-0232
Hammond R M 538ValleyProv ----272-4346
Hammond Ralph C
    171GainesvilleDrWrwk--738-9678
Hammond Raymond M
    18HedleyAvCF--728-5998
Hammond Richard BoswellRdFos --647-5365
Hammond Richard 135WillowProv -421-2931
Hammond Richard H
    41BreezyLakeDrCov--821-1396
Hammond Richard T
    18SunsetLnPlainvil --699-2660
Hammond Robt A
    202PawtcktAvPawt--727-0511
Hammond Robt A
    31WindsorRdPawt--726-6039
Hammond Robt P HarkneyHillRdCov 397-4063
Hammond Robt S 141VincntAvEPrv 434-0479
Hammond Roland Mrs
    41BoylstnAvProv--751-5949
Hammond Roland A 236PointProv 331-1783
Hammond Roland F
    18RockyRdAvLcln--726-0330
Hammond Ronald 196HuntAvWrwk 737-7921
Hammond Ronald C 84HelenAvWrwk 739-9364
Hammond Sally E 80MyrtleAvCrns 941-6056
Hammond Sanford L
    429CedarAvEGrn--884-4934
    Sum Res HarkneyHlRdCov ----397-7325
Hammond Susan F
    95MathewsonProv--331-7429
Hammond Thos
    258MontgomeryAvCrns--461-0730
Hammond Verla Gall 3BarnesProv --272-6392
Hammond Victoria B
    1112ReosvltAvPawt--723-7334
Hammond W Chas
    2065MinerlSprngAvNPrv--231-0664
Hammond Walter H DanlsnPikeFos 647-5686
Hammond Wm D 183PalmerAvWrwk 737-9236
Hammons Allen Jas
    501PottrsAvProv--941-9572
Hammontree Jas 398FairvwAvCov 821-8499
Hamod Geo 10ElmCmb ----------722-6540
Hamod Geo R Jr 244HarrietLnCmb -333-6265
Hamod Sarah Mrs 149WashCF ----726-0315
Hamolsky Milton W Dr
    150ArlngtnAvProv--861-2697
Hamor Donald A 20TifftNAtt ----695-5037
Hampden Shell Center
    239NewMeadwRdBar--245-9496
Hampshire Alfred E
    147CapronFarmDrWrwk--737-6424

EXAMPLE

Earl D. Hamilton ___245-1276___

You find Earl D. Hamilton's phone number under *Hamilton Earl D* in the directory.

Time for Items 1–10

Start

Finish

Time for Items 11–20

Start

Finish

Name or Business to Look Up	Telephone Number	Name or Business to Look Up	Telephone Number
1. Arthur Hamlin	1. ___	11. Ellery W. Hammarlund	11. ___
2. Howard Hamel	2. ___	12. David E. Hamilton	12. ___
3. Mrs. Rose Hamill	3. ___	13. H. J. Hamel	13. ___
4. Hamilton Hotel	4. ___	14. James W. Hammond, Jr.	14. ___
5. Alfred E. Hampshire	5. ___	15. Hampden Shell Center	15. ___
6. Hammart, Inc.	6. ___	16. Hamel Tool Company	16. ___
7. Joseph C. Hamilton	7. ___	17. Charles Hamer	17. ___
8. Laura Hamilton	8. ___	18. Peter Hammerschlag	18. ___
9. Hammond Motor Sales	9. ___	19. Hamilton Mills Army & Navy Store	19. ___
10. Frederick Hamilton, Optometrist	10. ___	20. James Hammontree	20. ___

ANSWER KEY: PAGE 137

Items 1–10 ▶	Scanning Time		Items 11–20 ▶	Scanning Time	
	Number Correct			Number Correct	

Scanning Indexes

An index is located in the back of many books. By scanning the index, you can find out if the book discusses a particular topic and, if so, on what pages the information is located.

The index lists alphabetically all important ideas or names for easy reference. Major subject headings will be followed by a list of pages containing a reference to that topic. Many indexes, like the one in this exercise, list various subtopics under the major subject headings along with the pages on which the subtopics can be found. Thus, in the following index, below the major subject heading *Compromises* are listed the subtopics *Compromises in the Constitution,* 119; the *Missouri Compromise,* 190, 221, 227; the *Compromise Tariff of 1833,* 210; and so on.

Often the pages having diagrams are indicated in an index. In the following index, italic type is used for the numbers of the pages containing illustrations and maps.

In addition to the above information, indexes often use cross references to direct the reader to related topics. Thus, in the following index, a reader looking up *Civil Service* will be told to *See also Spoils System.* If the major subject heading being looked up is too broad, a cross reference will refer you to more specific headings. For example, following the heading *Church* in the index for this exercise there are no page

numbers. Instead, a cross reference suggests that you look in the index under the major subject headings *Catholic Church* and *Religion.*

As a student you will find the index of a book a valuable tool. The following exercise will familiarize you with the use of an index as well as increase your efficiency at scanning this important study aid.

Directions: Take a few moments to become familiar with the arrangement of information in the index on page 90. Notice the major subject headings followed by page numbers. Note that subheadings follow the major headings and are indented. The subjects are arranged alphabetically, the first beginning with *a* and the last with *c.*

Complete the exercise on page 91 by scanning the index to locate the number of the page on which you will find the required information. As you locate each page number, write it in the blank provided. Study the example first.

You may want to time this exercise to see if you can increase your speed. Keep track of your time for each group of 15, and record your timings in the spaces provided.

Strive for 100 percent accuracy. When finished, correct your answers using the answer key on page 137. ▶

EXAMPLE

Stephen Austin   _639_

Information about Stephen Austin is located by looking up *Austin* in the index.

Time for Items 1–15

Start

Finish

Time for Items 16–30

Start

Finish

Information to Locate	Page	Information to Locate	Page
1. Civil Rights Bill	1. _____	16. Clara Barton	16. _____
2. Hernán Cortés	2. _____	17. Children's rights	17. _____
3. English "Bill of Rights"	3. _____	18. picture of Benedict Arnold	18. _____
4. picture of Andrew Carnegie	4. _____	19. the date Grover Cleveland was first elected President	19. _____
5. Crittenden Compromise	5. _____	20. "Boston Massacre"	20. _____
6. the growth of the Catholic church	6. _____	21. a definition of Bolshevism	21. _____
7. the definition of Communism	7. _____	22. map of California	22. _____
8. map of the physiographic features of America	8. _____	23. impressionistic art	23. _____
9. Second Continental Congress	9. _____	24. map of Connecticut	24. _____
10. quotation from James Bryce	10. _____	25. date the U.S. Constitution was ratified	25. _____
11. picture of Susan B. Anthony	11. _____	26. illustration of the Boston Tea Party	26. _____
12. Canada and the Oregon boundary	12. _____	27. crime in colonial days	27. _____
13. *Biglow Papers*	13. _____	28. Big Business and the New Deal	28. _____
14. Henry Clay's role in the Missouri Compromise	14. _____	29. "Blue Cross"	29. _____
15. a diagram illustrating investments in Canada	15. _____	30. a diagram illustrating checks and balances	30. _____

ANSWER KEY: PAGE 137

| Items 1–15 ▶ | Scanning Time | | Items 16–30 ▶ | Scanning Time | |
| Number Correct | | | Number Correct | | |

Scanning TV Listings

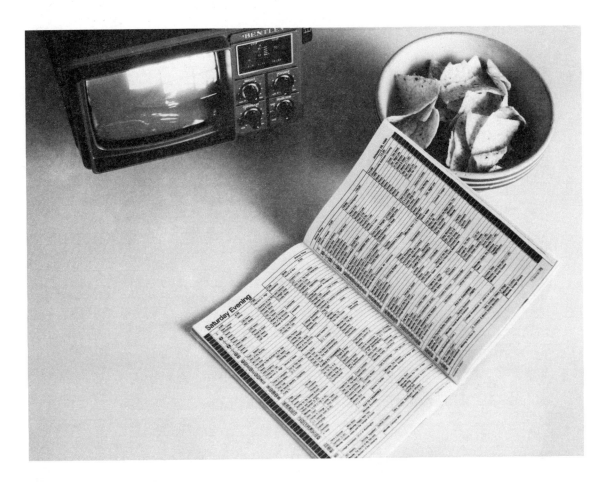

Every evening millions of people scan the TV program listings in their newspaper or TV magazine. Often they want to know when a particular program is being shown. Sometimes they want to know when a favorite star will appear or when a show on a particular topic will be presented.

More sophisticated TV viewers soon learn that the same show may be on at several different times, and hence, they can choose when they want to see it. Other shows might be on several different channels at the same time, and the viewer might select the channel having the best reception.

In any event, straight reading of the TV listings is seldom done; more often, skimming or scanning skills are employed. Use this exercise to sharpen and speed up your scanning.

Directions: Take a few moments to become familiar with the arrangement of information in the following TV page. It contains a Program Chart (6–9 P.M.) and more detailed listings (6–7 P.M.). Then read each question and scan for the answer. Record your answer in the blank provided. Study the example first.

It is both educationally sound and a lot of fun to do this exercise with another person or in a small group. Race to see who can find the answer first. Make each question a separate race. As you locate an answer, record it in the blank provided.

Correct each answer using the answer key on page 138 before going on to the next question. You may avoid the problem of seeing the answer to the next question either by having someone else look up the answer for you or by holding a card or piece of paper over the remaining answers. Strive for 100 percent accuracy. ▶

Sunday Evening

6 PM (2) NEWS; 60 min.

(3) WAR OF THE WORLDS—Science Fiction; 60 min.
A member of the alien triumvirate known as The Advocacy falls ill, and the need for brainpower reaches the crisis point. Sylvia: Ann Robinson. Harrison: Jared Martin.

(4) ENTERTAINMENT THIS WEEK—Magazine; 60 min.
Scheduled: Cyndi Lauper; Ben Vereen.

(5) HOLLYWOOD CHRISTMAS PARADE; 2 hrs.
Bob Eubanks and Lee Meriwether co-host the 57th annual strut down Sunset and Hollywood Boulevards, replete with floats, antique cars, marching bands and a cavalcade of celebrity participants. See the Close-up on A-74 for parade details. (Live)

(6) NBC NEWS—Garrick Utley

(7) NEWS

(11) WONDERFUL WORLD OF DISNEY; 60 min.
Eight cartoons find "Mickey and Donald Kidding Around" with their respective nephews.

(13) MOVIE—Crime Drama; 2 hrs. ★★
"Code of Silence." (1985) Action-packed hit with Chuck Norris as a loner cop and one-man army combatting gangsters in Chicago. Henry Silva, Bert Remsen. Luna: Mike Genovese.

(18) TAWAG NG TANGHALAN/PHILIPPINE'S BEST—In Tagalog

(24) COMPUTER CHRONICLES

(40) E.V. HILL—Religion

(50) NOVA (CC); 60 min.
Recalling a record-breaking 72-mile human-powered 1988 flight from Crete to Santorini.

(52) ESTRENOS Y ESTRELLAS—Magazine; 60 min.

(56) DOI MASARU OKAZUNO COOKING—In Japanese

(A&E) VANITY FAIR—Drama

(CBN) IN TOUCH—Religion; 60 min.

(CNN) WEEK IN REVIEW—Russell/Cain; 60 min.

(DSC) IN THE JAWS OF SATAN; 60 min.

(HBO) MOVIE—Adventure; 1 hr., 50 min. ★★★
"Jeremiah Johnson."

(LIF) INTERNAL MEDICINE UPDATE

(MTV) BON JOVI IS BACK!—Documentary

(NIK) KIDS' COURT—Children

(PT) WOMEN'S TENNIS
Martina Navratilova vs. Chris Evert in the Michelin Challenge at Inglewood, Cal. (Live)

(SHO) DIONNE WARWICK AND FRIENDS; 60 min.

(TBS) NATIONAL GEOGRAPHIC EXPLORER; 2 hrs.
A Swiss artist and amateur anthropologist who lives with a nomadic forest tribe in Borneo; the first French mountaineering expedition in Pakistan's Karakoram range in 1936.

(TNN) MOTOWORLD—Motorcycle Racing
The Western/Eastern Road Racing Grand National Finale, taped Nov. 12-13 at Atlanta.

(WGN) STAR SEARCH—Talent Contest; 60 min.

(WOR) UNTOUCHABLES (BW); 60 min.

6:05 (56) NEWS—In Japanese

6:30 (6) RUNAWAY WITH THE RICH AND FAMOUS
Donna Mills travels to Yugoslavia.

(7) SISKEL & EBERT
Scheduled: "Scrooged" (Bill Murray, Karen Allen); "Cocoon: The Return."

(18) DA PROFESSIONALS—In Tagalog

(MAX) MOVIE—Comedy; 1 hr., 35 min. ★
"Morgan Stewart's Coming Home."

(MTV) WEEK IN ROCK

(NIK) LOONEY TUNES—Cartoon

(TNN) HIDDEN HEROES—Auto Racing
World of Outlaws sprint-car racer Sammy Swindel is profiled.

6:35 (56) HOLLYWOOD 1001 NIGHTS—In Japanese

7 PM (2) 60 MINUTES (CC); 60 min.

(4) (6) MAGICAL WORLD OF DISNEY (CC)—Comedy; 60 min.
Harry Anderson plays "The Absent-Minded Professor," a cheerful eccentric who re-creates flubber, the antigravity flying rubber that

(24) TELECOMMUNICATIONS AND INFORMATION REVOLUTION
The conclusion of a two-part discussion of public broadcasting. (Repeat)

(28) LIGHT OF THE GODS—Documentary
Tracing Greek art from the 9th to the 5th century B.C., a time when it evolved from abstract human representations to realistic forms. Viewed: Theran wall paintings.

(34) NOTICIERO UNIVISION—Ramos/Salinas

(40) LLOYD OGILVIE—Religion

(A&E) DIARY OF ANNE FRANK—Drama

(LIF) OBSTETRICS/GYNECOLOGY UPDATE

Prime Time

	6:00	6:30	7:00	7:30	8:00	8:30
(2)	News		60 Minutes		Murder, She Wrote	
(3)	War of the Worlds		Incredible Sunday		Mission: Impossible	
(4)	Entertainment This Week		Magical World of Disney		Family Ties	Day by Day
(5)	Hollywood Christmas Parade				Faerie Tale Theatre	
(6)	NBC News	Runaway/ Famous	Magical World of Disney		Family Ties	Day by Day
(7)	News	Siskel & Ebert	Incredible Sunday		Mission: Impossible	
(9)	Movie: The Bounty (5:00)		Movie: Harry & Son			
(11)	Wonderful World of Disney		21 Jump Street		Most Wanted	Married...
(13)	Movie: Code of Silence				Movie: Hang 'Em High	
(18)	Tawag Ng Tanghalan	Da Professionals	El Noticiero	Money Talks	Shadow Warriors IV	
(24)	Computer Chronicles	Telecom-munications	Upstairs, Downstairs		Masterpiece Theatre	
(28)	The Mind (5:30)	Light of the Gods	Last Bastion	Videolog (7:50)	Nature	
(34)	Deportes (5:30)	Noticiero	Película: Nora la rebelde			
(40)	E.V. Hill	Lloyd Ogilvie	Kenneth Copeland		Praise the Lord	
(50)	Nova		Nature		Masterpiece Theatre	
(52)	Estrenos...		Charytin		Película: La hora del jaguar	
(56)	News (6:05)	H'wood Nights (6:35)	Tokuso Saizensen		Hollywood Park	Let's Talk
(58)	L.A.U.S.D. Committee (5:00)	Off the air				

CABLE-TV CHANNELS

	6:00	6:30	7:00	7:30	8:00	8:30
(A&E)	Vanity Fair	Anne Frank	Rich Little		When... Rotten	French/Saunders
(CBN)	In Touch		Changed Lives	John Ankerberg	Outdoorsman	Ed Young
(CNN)	Week in Review		News		Int'l Correspond.	Sports
(DSC)	In the Jaws of Satan		Stranded		Yap, How'd You Know We'd Like TV	
(ESN)	NFL Football: Giants at Saints (5:00)				SportsCenter	
(LIF)	Internal Medicine	OB/Gyn. Update	Gallstone Therapy	Milestones	Physicians' Journal Update	
(NIK)	Kids' Court	Looney Tunes	Inspector Gadget	Count Duckula	Mister Ed	Patty Duke
(PT)	Women's Tennis: Evert vs. Navratilova					
(TBS)	Nat'l Geographic Explorer				All in the Family	Jerry Falwell
(TNN)	Motoworld	Hidden Heroes	Celebrity Outdoors	America's Horse	Rodeo	
(USA)	Thanks for Giving (4:00)					
(WGN)	Star Search		News		Instant Replay (7:40)	Monsters	Magnum, P.I.
(WOR)	Untouchables		News		D.C. Follies	11-22-63: The Day the Nation Cried

PAY-TV CHANNELS

	6:00	6:30	7:00	7:30	8:00	8:30
(DIS)	Movie: Three Amigos! (5:00)		Movie: Please Don't Eat the Daisies			
(HBO)	Movie: Jeremiah Johnson				Dangerous Life	
(MAX)	Movie: Walk, Don't Run (4:30)	Movie: Morgan Stewart's Coming Home			Movie: Project X	
(SEL)	Movie: Trouble w/Spies (5:00)		Movie: The Untouchables			
(SHO)	Dionne Warwick and Friends		Movie: Surrender			
(TMC)	Movie: Three for the Road (5:30)		Movie: Tough Guys Don't Dance			
(Z)	Movie: Shenandoah (5:00)		Movie: Like Father, like Son			

Cable/Pay-TV

(A&E) Arts & Entertainment Network	(ESN) ESPN	(NIK) Nickelodeon	(TNN) The Nashville Network
(CBN) CBN Family Channel	(HBO) Home Box Office	(PT) Prime Ticket Network	(USA) USA Network
(CNN) Cable News Network	(LIF) Lifetime	(SHO) Showtime	(WGN) WGN (Chicago; Ind.)
(DIS) The Disney Channel	(MAX) Cinemax	(TBS) TBS	(WOR) WWOR (New Jersey; Ind.)
(DSC) The Discovery Channel	(MTV) Music Television	(TMC) The Movie Channel	(Z) Z Channel

EXAMPLE
What program is on Channel 4 at 7:00? __Magical__

__World of Disney__

Note: Use the Program Chart first and the full listing for details if needed.

Time for Entire Drill

Start

Finish

Time for Each Item

1. Which channels have news at 6:00? _____

2. Which channel has shows especially for doctors? _____

3. What time does "Nature" come on? _____

4. What is "National Geographic Explorer"? _____

_____

5. Which channels have programs in Spanish? _____

6. If you understood only Japanese, which channel news would you listen to?

_____

7. Is CNN (Cable News Network) a pay TV channel? _____

8. What kind of show is "Vanity Fair"? _____

9. In which country do the people speak Tagalog? _____

10. How long does the program "21 Jump Street" last? _____

11. What time does the movie *Tough Guys Don't Dance* come on? _____

12. Who are the stars in "Women's Tennis"? _____

_____

1. _____ seconds

2. _____ seconds

3. _____ seconds

4. _____ seconds

5. _____ seconds

6. _____ seconds

7. _____ seconds

8. _____ seconds

9. _____ seconds

10. _____ seconds

11. _____ seconds

12. _____ seconds

ANSWER KEY: PAGE 138

Number Correct

Scanning Time

Scanning Train Schedules

Passenger trains have been around for over a hundred years. While they are not as popular a mode of transportation as they were several decades ago, there are still hundreds of thousands of people who ride them every week.

In any event, train schedules are similar to bus and airline schedules, and every educated person should know how to scan them accurately and rapidly. They are loaded with a variety of travel information.

Besides just giving times, schedules tell you which trains run between which towns and on what days. With simple subtraction, you can find out which trains are fastest, and by counting you can tell how many stops they make. If the schedule doesn't give the time for a stop, the train doesn't stop there. As a bit of additional information, the schedule gives the miles the train travels from the point of origin.

In most cases, the purpose of scanning a train schedule is simply to answer a specific question. It can be both boring and unnecessary to read the entire schedule since it is unlikely that you will be going to all of the cities and towns listed on it. Thus, your scanning ability becomes very useful for this type of material.

If you are not familiar with train schedules, it will take you a few moments to figure out how to get the desired information. However, once you become familiar with the arrangement of the schedule, you will be able to answer the questions in the following exercise easily and quickly.

In this exercise accuracy is more important than speed, but don't dillydally. You don't want to be slowly reading the schedule in the station as the train is pulling out.

Directions: Take a moment to look over the whole schedule. Look carefully at the headings of the columns. Notice the destinations of the various trains.

Read each of the following questions and scan the schedule to locate the answer. Do each question as if it were the only bit of information you needed. Don't try to do several at once. Record each answer in the blank provided. Study the example first.

Try to increase your speed as you go along but do not sacrifice accuracy. You may wish to time yourself with a stopwatch for each question. Start the watch as soon as you begin to scan the schedule, and stop the watch when you have located the answer. Do not time the period it takes you to record your answer. Record your scanning time in the space provided. As you begin to scan for the next answer, try to improve on your previous speed.

When you have completed the exercise, find your total scanning time. You may want to compare your total time with that of other members of your class.

When finished, correct your answers using the answer key on page 138. If you made any errors, turn back to the question and the schedule to discover what you did wrong. Errors in reading a train schedule are more serious than many reading comprehension errors; you could miss the train or end up in the wrong city. ▶

EASTERN STANDARD TIME

WASHINGTON — BALTIMORE — WILMINGTON — PHILADELPHIA — TRENTON — NEWARK — NEW YORK — NEW HAVEN — HARTFORD — SPRINGFIELD — PROVIDENCE — BOSTON

Train Number		110	174	174/142	212	150	184	114	144	176	116
Train Name		*(Metroliner)*	The States-Man	Connecticut Yankee		The Flying Yankee	The Nar-ragansett	*(Metroliner)*	The Bankers	The Senator	*(Metroliner)*
Frequency of Operation		Mon-Sat	Daily	Daily	Mon-Sat	Mon-Fri	Sun Only	Daily	Daily	Daily	Daily
Station	**Miles from Washington →**										
WASHINGTON, DC .... Dp	0	11 00 a	11 05 a	11 05 a						1 05 p	2 00 p
Capitol Beltway Station, MD (Lanham)	9	11 10 a								1 18 p	
BALTIMORE, MD (Penn. Sta.)	40	11 36 a	11 46 a	11 46 a						1 49 p	2 32 p
WILMINGTON, DE.	108	12 21 p	12 47 p	12 47 p						2 49 p	3 18 p
PHILADELPHIA, PA (30th St. Sta.)	134	12 45 p	1 15 p	1 15 p	2 15 p		2 15 p	2 42 p		3 15 p	3 42 p
North Philadelphia, PA	138		1 25 p	1 25 p	2 25 p		2 25 p				
TRENTON, NJ	166	1 12 p	1 52 p	1 52 p	2 53 p		2 53 p	3 09 p		3 52 p	
Princeton Jct. (Princeton ◆)	175										
New Brunswick	191										
Metropark (Iselin)	199										
NEWARK, NJ (Penn. Sta.)	214		2 40 p	2 40 p	3 40 p		3 40 p	d 3 45 p		4 40 p	
NEW YORK, NY (Penn. Sta.) .... Ar	224	2 02 p	2 55 p	2 55 p	3 55 p		3 55 p	4 03 p		4 55 p	
NEW YORK, NY (Penn. Sta.) .... Dp	224		3 10 p	3 10 p		4 10 p	4 10 p		4 50 p	5 10 p	
Rye, NY	251								5 43 p		
Stamford, CT	260		4 00 p	4 00 p					6 11 p		
Bridgeport	282		4 25 p	4 25 p					6 29 p		
NEW HAVEN .... Ar	299		4 45 p	4 45 p		5 38 p	5 38 p		6 39 p	6 42 p	
NEW HAVEN .... Dp	299		4 55 p	5 00 p		5 38 p	5 48p		6 58 p	6 52 p	
Wallingford *(Via Inland Route)*	312			5 19 p					7 08 p		
Meriden	318			5 30 p					7 18 p		
Berlin (New Britain)	325			5 41 p					7 31 p		
HARTFORD	336			5 55 p							
Windsor	342			6 03 p							
Windsor Locks	348			6 11 p					d 7 46 p		
Thompsonville, CT (Enfield)	353			6 19 p							
SPRINGFIELD, MA	361			6 37 p					8 10 p		
Old Saybrook, CT	332		5 48 p			6 10 p	6 22 p			7 45 p	
New London	350					6 30 p	6 43 p			7 56 p	
Mystic, CT (Mystic Seaport)	359					7 26 p	7 43 p			8 47 p	
Westerly, RI	368					d 8 03 p	8 18 p			9 20 p	
Kingston	385					d 8 18 p	d 8 35 p			d 9 35 p	
PROVIDENCE, RI	412		6 48 p			8 25 p	8 40 p			9 40 p	
Route 128, MA	444		7 21 p								
BOSTON (Back Bay Sta.)	455		d 7 35 p								
BOSTON, MA (South Sta.) .... Ar	456		7 40 p								

Notes on service: Columns 110, 114, 116 — **METROLINER**. Column 144 — **NOW! PARLOR CAR SERVICE**. Column 176 — **AMFLEET SERVICE**.

🚆 Metroliner

EXAMPLE

The Senator

What is the name of the train that leaves Washington, D.C. at 1:05?

Time for Entire Drill

Start

Finish

Answer

1. _____ _____
2. _____
3. _____
4. _____
5. _____
6. _____
7. _____
8. _____
9. _____
10. _____
11. _____
12. _____
13. _____
14. _____
15. _____

Question

1. What are the numbers of the two trains which go from Washington to Boston?
2. Which one arrives in Boston earlier?
3. Find the number of the train which runs between Philadelphia and New York only.
4. What time does The Flying Yankee leave New York?
5. What time does The Flying Yankee get to Boston South Station?
6. Does The Flying Yankee stop in Stamford, Connecticut?
7. What time does the Connecticut Yankee get to New Haven?
8. How far is Trenton from Washington?
9. How many days per week does The Narragansett run?
10. How many days per week does Metroliner No. 110 run?
11. How long does it take The Flying Yankee to get from New York (Penn Sta.) to Boston (South Sta.)?
12. How long does it take The Narragansett to cover the same route?
13. If you miss the 11:00 A.M. train from Washington to Baltimore, when is the next train?
14. How much later will you arrive in Baltimore if you have to take the next train?
15. If you were riding from Washington to Boston on The Statesman, how long would the train stop in New York?

Time for Each Item

1. _____ seconds
2. _____ seconds
3. _____ seconds
4. _____ seconds
5. _____ seconds
6. _____ seconds
7. _____ seconds
8. _____ seconds
9. _____ seconds
10. _____ seconds
11. _____ seconds
12. _____ seconds
13. _____ seconds
14. _____ seconds
15. _____ seconds

ANSWER KEY: PAGE 138

Number Correct

Scanning Time

Scanning Best-Seller Lists

If you want to know what the best-selling book in the country is, you can find out by looking at lists of best sellers which appear in major newspapers around the country. Two of the best known are the lists which appear every Sunday in the *New York Times Book Review* and in the *Los Angeles Times*. *The Book Review*, a section of the Sunday paper, is available at many libraries around the country. Another list that is widely read appears in *Publishers Weekly*, a magazine which also can be found in most libraries.

There is a surprisingly large amount of information in a list such as this. Following the first entry you will find the author, the publisher, the price, a brief description of contents, the book's rank this week, the book's rank last week, and the number of weeks the book has been on the list. The list is divided into two parts: Fiction and Nonfiction. The following exercise will familiarize you with the type of information found on best-seller lists while you improve your scanning ability. When scanning this type of material, strive for speed and accuracy.

Directions: Take a few moments to become familiar with the organization of the information contained in the best-seller list on page 102. Then read each question and scan for the answer. Record your answer in the blank provided. Study the example first.

You may choose to do this exercise with another person or in a small group. Race to see who can find the answer first. Make each question a separate race. As you locate each answer, record it in the blank provided.

Correct each answer using the answer key on page 138 before going on to the next question. Avoid the problem of seeing the answer to the next question either by having someone else look up the answer for you or by holding a card or piece of paper over the remaining answers. Strive for 100 percent accuracy. ▶

Ranking This Week	Fiction	Ranking Last Week	Weeks on List
1	THE QUEEN OF THE DAMNED: The Third Book in the Vampire Chronicles by Anne Rice. (Alfred A. Knopf: $18.95.) Living dead mix it up with living in a dark walk in history.	2	5
2	ONE by Richard Bach. (Silver Arrow/William Morrow: $17.95.) Bach and his wife take a fantasy trip to meet their younger selves and also to consider alternate paths.	6	3
3	ANYTHING FOR BILLY by Larry McMurtry. (Simon & Schuster: $18.95.) McMurtry treats the Billy-the-Kid legend.	3	5
4	THE CARDINAL OF THE KREMLIN by Tom Clancy. (G. P. Putnam's Sons: $19.95.) The Star Wars defense race places a Soviet spy's life on the line and war or peace in the balance.	1	16
5	THE SANDS OF TIME by Sidney Sheldon. (William Morrow: $19.95.) Nuns become enmeshed in the clashes between a Basque revolutionary and a Spanish army colonel.	—	1
6	BREATHING LESSONS by Anne Tyler. (Alfred A. Knopf: $18.95.) A trip to a funeral becomes a trip through marriage.	4	8
7	FINAL FLIGHT by Stephen Coonts. (Doubleday: $18.95.) A terrorist wants nuclear weapons but gets a dogfight with "Flight of the Intruder" hero Jake Grafton.	7	5
8	DRAGONSDAWN by Anne McCaffrey. (Del Rey/Ballantine: $18.95.) Planet Pern will be spore-spoiled unless fire-breathing, dragonlike lizards bulk up to dragon size.	9	2
9	LOVE IN THE TIME OF CHOLERA by Gabriel Garcia Márquez; translated from Spanish by Edith Grossman. (Alfred A. Knopf: $18.95.) A long-unrequited love may finally glow on a cholera-quarantined boat.	5	29
10	ALASKA by James A. Michener. (Random House: $22.50.) This historical fiction traces development of the 49th state.	8	20

Nonfiction

1	THE LAST LION: Winston Spencer Churchill, Alone, 1932–1940 by William Manchester. (Little, Brown: $24.95.) Churchill stands against Nazi aggression while being rejected at home.	1	4
2	A BRIEF HISTORY OF TIME: From the Big Bang to Black Holes by Stephen W. Hawking. (Bantam Books: $18.95.) Hawking makes fundamental questions of the universe accessible.	3	30
3	THE 8-WEEK CHOLESTEROL CURE: How to Lower Your Blood Cholesterol by Up to 40 Percent Without Drugs or Deprivation by Robert E. Kowalski. (Harper & Row: $15.95.) What you eat is as important as what you avoid.	2	49
4	CHILD STAR by Shirley Temple Black. (McGraw-Hill : $19.95.) Black describes the life behind her childhood in film.	4	3
5	THE FIRST SALUTE by Barbara W. Tuchman. (Alfred A. Knopf: $22.95.) Tuchman reconstructs the U.S. journey to nationhood.	7	6
6	A BRIGHT SHINING LIE: John Paul Vann and America in Vietnam by Neil Sheehan. (Random House: $24.95.) Sheehan combines Vann's life with history for a different look at the Vietnam War.	5	3
7	GOLDWATER by Barry M. Goldwater with Jack Casserly. (Doubleday: $21.95.) Goldwater remembers four decades in politics.	8	3
8	SWIM WITH THE SHARKS WITHOUT BEING EATEN ALIVE: Outsell, Outmanage, Outmotivate & Outnegotiate Your Competition by Harvey Mackay. (William Morrow: $15.95.) Mackay sells his way for you to get successful.	—	31
9	THE RAGMAN'S SON by Kirk Douglas. (Simon & Schuster: $21.95.) Douglas describes his rise from poverty to acting success.	—	12
10	ALL YOU CAN DO IS ALL YOU CAN DO: But All You Can Do Is Enough by A. L. Williams. (Oliver-Nelson: $14.95.) In$urance aleman William$ ha$ a new life for you.	—	6

EXAMPLE

James A. Michener   Who wrote *Alaska*?

Time for Entire Drill

Start

Finish

Answer

1. _____

2. _____

3. _____

4. _____

5. _____

6. _____

7. _____

8. _____

9. _____

10. _____

11. _____

12. _____

13. _____

_____

14. _____

15. _____

Question

1. What is the best-selling fiction title this week?

2. Who wrote the best-selling nonfiction book?

3. On the fiction list, the book that is now Number 8 was in what position last week?

4. Who published *Child Star*?

5. What is *Anything for Billy* about?

6. In which list is *A Bright Shining Lie*?

7. What person is *The Ragman's Son* about?

8. How many weeks has *The 8-Week Cholesterol Cure* been on the list of best-sellers?

9. Which book has moved up in popularity the most from last week?

10. Which book is new in the fiction list this week?

11. What book is published by Bantam Books?

12. How much does *Goldwater* sell for?

13. Which books are about movie stars?

14. Which book did Anne McCaffrey write?

15. Which book has been on the list the longest?

Time for Each Item

1. _____ seconds

2. _____ seconds

3. _____ seconds

4. _____ seconds

5. _____ seconds

6. _____ seconds

7. _____ seconds

8. _____ seconds

9. _____ seconds

10. _____ seconds

11. _____ seconds

12. _____ seconds

13. _____ seconds

14. _____ seconds

15. _____ seconds

ANSWER KEY: PAGE 138

Number Correct   Scanning Time

Scanning Hit-Record Charts

read. Like book best-seller lists, they contain a lot of information. Before you can begin to scan, you must take a few minutes to understand the arrangement of this information.

Let's take a look at the music charts shown on pages 106, 108, 110, and 112. The first chart lists the top 23 songs from the *Billboard* "Hot 100 Singles." The songs are ranked in order of popularity for the week. Let's read the first one together. The circle around Number 1 in the first column means that the song has risen in popularity during the week. Last week it was Number 2, and it has been on the chart for 13 weeks. The title is "Wild, Wild West" and the artist or star performer in this instance is The Escape Club.

The second line of the song's listing gives the producer, the writer (in parentheses), the record label, and producing company number. In some instances there is a distributing label, which means that another company acts as distributor. For example, the Number 14 record "Don't Know What You Got" has a Mercury label, but it is distributed by Polygram. This means that if you want the record ordered for you, the store must get it from Polygram, not from the producing company Mercury.

The charts in the following exercises are all arranged in a similar way. Knowing this will help you scan them with speed and accuracy.

Directions: The following exercise will give you practice in scanning a music chart. Read the first question in Part A. Then scan for the answer in Chart A, *Billboard* "Hot 100 Singles." The answers to all questions in Part A can be located in Chart A. When you locate an answer, write it in the blank provided. Study the example first.

When scanning, strive for speed and accuracy. This exercise may be done with another person or in a small group. Race to see who can find the answer first. After you record your answer, correct it using the answer key on page 138 before going on to the next question. Be sure, however, to avoid seeing the answers to the remaining questions.

When you have completed Part A, go on to Part B, C, and D. Your goal for all exercises should be 100 percent accuracy. ▶

If you are interested in popular music or what record is "hot," a good source is *Billboard,* a weekly newspaper magazine. This is where disc jockeys get their chatter and selections, where record stores find out what to order, and where recording stars find out if the public loves them.

But the music charts are not always so easy to

Billboard® HOT 100® SINGLES™

THIS WEEK	LAST WEEK	2 WKS. AGO	WKS. ON CHART	TITLE PRODUCER (SONGWRITER)	ARTIST LABEL & NUMBER/DISTRIBUTING LABEL
				Compiled from a national sample of retail store and one-stop sales reports and radio playlists.	
				★★ No. 1 ★★	
(1)	2	3	13	**WILD, WILD WEST** 1 week at No. One C. KIMSEY (THE ESCAPE CLUB)	◆THE ESCAPE CLUB (T) (C) ATLANTIC 7-89048
2	1	2	11	**KOKOMO (FROM THE "COCKTAIL" SOUNDTRACK)** T.MELCHER (M.LOVE, T.MELCHER, J. PHILLIPS, S.MACKENZIE)	◆THE BEACH BOYS (C) ELEKTRA 7-69385
(3)	4	7	12	**THE LOCO-MOTION** STOCK, AITKEN, WATERMAN (G.GOFFIN, C.KING)	◆KYLIE MINOGUE (T) (C) GEFFEN 7-27752
(4)	5	10	8	**BAD MEDICINE** B.FAIRBAIRN (J. BON JOVI, R. SAMBORA, D. CHILD)	◆BON JOVI (C) (D) MERCURY 870 657-7/POLYGRAM
5	6	9	10	**ONE MOMENT IN TIME** NARADA (A.HAMMOND, J. BETTIS)	◆WHITNEY HOUSTON (C) ARISTA 1-9743
(6)	8	14	7	**DESIRE** J.IOVINE (BONO, U2)	◆U2 (T) (C) ISLAND 7-99250/ATLANTIC
7	3	1	11	**GROOVY KIND OF LOVE** P.COLLINS, A.DUDLEY (T.WINE, C.BAYER BACHARACH)	◆PHIL COLLINS (T) (C) ATLANTIC 7-89017
(8)	13	21	10	**BABY, I LOVE YOUR WAY/FREEBIRD MEDLEY** B.ROSENBERG (P.FRAMPTON, A.COLLINS, R.VAN ZANDT)	◆WILL TO POWER (C) EPIC 34-08034/E.P.A.
(9)	15	22	6	**KISSING A FOOL** G.MICHAEL (G.MICHAEL)	◆GEORGE MICHAEL (T) (C) (CD) COLUMBIA 38-08050
10	7	8	14	**NEVER TEAR US APART** C.THOMAS (A.FARRISS, M.HUTCHENCE)	◆INXS (T) (C) (M) ATLANTIC 7-89038
(11)	12	17	10	**HOW CAN I FALL?** B.SARGEANT (D.GLASPER, M.LILLINGTON)	◆BREATHE (C) A&M 1224
(12)	17	23	8	**LOOK AWAY** R.NEVISON (D.WARREN)	◆CHICAGO (C) (CD) REPRISE 7-27766
(13)	16	16	13	**ANOTHER LOVE** G.COLE (CAMPSIE, G.MCFARLANE, G.COLE)	◆GIANT STEPS (T) (C) A&M 1226
(14)	18	20	11	**DON'T KNOW WHAT YOU GOT (TILL IT'S GONE)** A.JOHNS, T.KEIFER, E.BRITTINGHAM (T.KEIFER)	◆CINDERELLA (C) MERCURY 870 644-7/POLYGRAM
(15)	20	27	5	**I DON'T WANT YOUR LOVE** DURAN DURAN, J.ELIAS, D.ABRAHAM (J.TAYLOR, N.RHODES, S.LEBON)	◆DURAN DURAN (T) (C) (CD) CAPITOL 44237
(16)	22	28	8	**GIVING YOU THE BEST THAT I GOT** M.POWELL (A.BAKER, S.SCARBOROUGH, R.HOLLAND)	◆ANITA BAKER (C) (CD) ELEKTRA 7-69371
(17)	23	29	10	**WAITING FOR A STAR TO FALL** A.MARDIN (G.MERRILL, S.RUBICAM)	◆BOY MEETS GIRL (C) RCA 8691
18	10	5	18	**WHAT'S ON YOUR MIND (PURE ENERGY)** F.MAHER (P.ROBB, K.VALAQUEN)	◆INFORMATION SOCIETY (T) (C) (M) TOMMY BOY 7-27826/REPRISE
(19)	24	25	9	**A WORD IN SPANISH** C.THOMAS (E.JOHN, B.TAUPIN)	◆ELTON JOHN (C) MCA 53408
20	9	4	29	**RED RED WINE** UB40, R.FALCONE (N.DIAMOND)	◆UB4O (C) A&M 1244
(21)	26	32	7	**WALK ON WATER** R.ZITO, E.MONEY (J.HARMS)	◆EDDIE MONEY (C) (CD) COLUMBIA 38-08060
(22)	27	33	11	**THE PROMISE** B.ROGAN (C.FARRINGTON, M.FLOREALE, A.MANN)	◆WHEN IN ROME (T) (C) VIRGIN 7-99323
23	11	6	13	**DON'T YOU KNOW WHAT THE NIGHT CAN DO?** S.WINWOOD, T.LORD-ALGE (S.WINWOOD, W.JENNINGS)	◆STEVE WINWOOD (T) (C) VIRGIN 7-99290

EXAMPLE

Kylie Minogue

Who is the artist for "The Loco-Motion?"

Time for Entire Drill

Start

Finish

Answer

1. _____

2. _____

3. _____

4. _____

5. _____

6. _____

7. _____

8. _____

9. _____

10. _____

Question

1. What record is Number 4 this week?

2. Where was (what rank) "How Can I Fall" last week?

3. What record is Number 19 this week?

4. What record has been on the chart the longest?

5. Who wrote "Red Red Wine"?

6. Who produced "One Moment in Time"?

7. What record was Number 1 two weeks ago?

8. What is the newest record on the chart?

9. Who is the artist for "Kokomo"?

10. What rank was Anita Baker's record last week?

Time for Each Item

1. _____ seconds

2. _____ seconds

3. _____ seconds

4. _____ seconds

5. _____ seconds

6. _____ seconds

7. _____ seconds

8. _____ seconds

9. _____ seconds

10. _____ seconds

ANSWER KEY: PAGE 138

Number Correct

Scanning Time

Billboard HOT LATIN TRACKS™

THIS WEEK	LAST WEEK	2 WKS. AGO	WKS. ON CHART	ARTIST LABEL	TITLE
					Compiled from national Latin radio airplay reports.
					★★ No. 1 ★★
1	1	1	11	ANGELA CARRASCO EMI	◆BOCA ROSA 4 weeks at No. One
2	2	5	6	ROBERTO CARLOS CBS	◆SI EL AMOR SE VA
3	4	4	10	YOLANDITA MONGE CBS	◆ESTE AMOR QUE HAY QUE CALLAR
4	7	10	5	ROCIO DURCAL ARIOLA	COMO TU MUJER
5	8	7	14	EMMANUEL RCA	◆QUE SERA
6	3	2	19	FRANCO PEERLESS	MARIA
7	5	3	15	E. GORME Y R. CARLOS CBS	SENTADO A LA VERA DEL CAMINO
8	9	6	11	VERONICA CASTRO PROFONO	MALA NOCHE NO
9	10	9	14	ISABEL PANTOJA RCA	◆HAZME TUYA UNA VEZ MAS
10	6	8	18	MARISELA MCA	YA NO
11	15	14	14	RAPHAEL CBS	◆SIEMPRE ESTAS DICIENDO QUE TE VAS
12	21	16	8	BRAULIO CBS	UNA MUJER COMO TU
13	11	11	24	LUCIA MENDEZ ARIOLA	◆ES UN ALMA EN PENA
14	13	22	5	CHARYTIN CHAR	◆ESE HOMBRE
15	17	17	9	MAX TORRES EMI	CARA DURA
16	16	21	7	LUPITA D'ALESSIO CBS	EL QUE JUEGA CON FUEGO
17	18	18	6	GILBERTO SANTAROSA COMBO	TU
18	12	12	13	YURI EMI	◆CUANDO BAJA LA MAREA
19	22	24	5	ALBERTO VASQUEZ/JOAN SEBASTIAN MUSART	MARACAS
20	14	13	13	LUIS ENRIQUE CBS	◆TU NO LE AMAS LE TEMES

EXAMPLE

Angela Carrasco   Which artist was Number 1 last week?

Time for Entire Drill

Start [ ]

Finish [ ]

Answer

1. _____
2. _____
3. _____
4. _____
5. _____
6. _____
7. _____
8. _____
9. _____
10. _____

Question

1. What song (title) was Number 5 this week?
2. What is the label for this week's Number 10 song?
3. What song did Max Torres sing?
4. Who sang "Ese Hombre"?
5. What song has been on the chart the longest?
6. What did Marisela sing?
7. Which artist was Number 13 two weeks ago?
8. Emmanuel's song is on what label?
9. Where is the song "Maria" this week?
10. What record climbed highest since last week?

Time for Each Item

1. _____ seconds
2. _____ seconds
3. _____ seconds
4. _____ seconds
5. _____ seconds
6. _____ seconds
7. _____ seconds
8. _____ seconds
9. _____ seconds
10. _____ seconds

ANSWER KEY: PAGE 138

Number Correct [ ]   Scanning Time [ ]

Billboard® HOT COUNTRY SINGLES™

THIS WEEK	LAST WEEK	2 WKS. AGO	WKS. ON CHART	Compiled from a national sample of radio playlists. TITLE / PRODUCER (SONGWRITER)	ARTIST / LABEL & NUMBER/DISTRIBUTING LABEL
★★ No. 1 ★★ 1 week at No. One					
1	3	4	14	**RUNAWAY TRAIN** R.CROWELL (J.STEWART)	◆ROSANNE CASH COLUMBIA 38-07988/CBS
2	4	6	15	**NEW SHADE OF BLUE** SOUTHERN PACIFIC, J.E.NORMAN (J.MCFEE, A.PESSIS)	SOUTHERN PACIFIC WARNER BROS. 7-27790
3	8	9	10	**I'LL LEAVE THIS WORLD LOVING YOU** S.BUCKINGHAM (W.KEMP)	◆RICKY VAN SHELTON COLUMBIA 38-08022/CBS
4	9	10	11	**I'VE BEEN LOOKIN'** J.LEO (J.IBBOTSON, J.HANNA)	NITTY GRITTY DIRT BAND WARNER BROS. 7-22750
5	11	13	10	**I KNOW HOW HE FEELS** J.BOWEN, R.MCENTIRE (R.BOWLES, W.ROBINSON)	◆REBA MCENTIRE MCA 53402
6	12	15	9	**IF YOU AIN'T LOVIN' (YOU AIN'T LIVIN')** J.BOWEN, G.STRAIT (T.COLLINS)	GEORGE STRAIT MCA 53400
7	13	16	13	**I WISH THAT I COULD FALL IN LOVE TODAY** T.COLLINS, F.FOSTER (H.HOWARD)	BARBARA MANDRELL CAPITOL 44220
8	15	18	12	**CHISELED IN STONE** B.MONTGOMERY (V.GOSDIN, M.D.BARNES)	VERN GOSDIN COLUMBIA 38-08003/CBS
9	16	19	12	**THAT'S THAT** B.MAHER (H.PRESTWOOD)	◆MICHAEL JOHNSON RCA 8650-7
10	7	8	14	**DESPERATELY** D.WILLIAMS, G. FUNDIS (J.O'HARA, K.WELCH)	DON WILLIAMS CAPITOL 44216
11	20	23	8	**A TENDER LIE** T.DUBOIS, S.HENDRICKS, RESTLESS HEART (R.SHARP)	◆RESTLESS HEART RCA 8714-7
12	19	22	9	**WHEN YOU SAY NOTHING AT ALL** G.FUNDIS, K.WHITLEY (P.OVERSTREET, D.SCHLITZ)	◆KEITH WHITLEY RCA 8637-7
13	18	21	11	**REBELS WITHOUT A CLUE** J.BOWEN, J.STROUD (D.BELLAMY)	THE BELLAMY BROTHERS MCA/CURB 53399/MCA
14	1	2	16	**DARLENE** R.CHANCEY (GEIGER, MULLIS, RECTOR)	T. GRAHAM BROWN CAPITOL 44205
15	2	3	16	**SUMMER WIND** P.WORLEY, E.SEAY (C.HILLMAN. S.HILL)	◆THE DESERT ROSE BAND MCA/CURB 53354/MCA
16	6	7	15	**WHAT DO YOU WANT FROM ME THIS TIME** B.LLOYD, R.FOSTER (R.FOSTER, B.LLOYD)	◆FOSTER AND LLOYD RCA 8633-7
17	10	12	13	**BOOGIE WOOGIE FIDDLE COUNTRY BLUES** J.STROUD (C.DANIELS, T.DIGREGARIO, T.CRAIN, C.HAYWARD, J.GAVIN)	◆THE CHARLIE DANIELS BAND EPIC 34-08002/CBS
18	5	5	15	**BLUE TO THE BONE** S.BUCKINGHAM (M.GARVIN, B.JONES)	SWEETHEARTS OF THE RODEO COLUMBIA 38-07985/CBS
19	23	27	8	**LOVE HELPS THOSE** J.STROUD (P.OVERSTREET)	PAUL OVERSTREET MTM 72113
20	25	28	9	**SPANISH EYES** C.MOMAN (B.KAEMPERT, C.SINGLETON, E.SNYDER)	◆WILLIE NELSON COLUMBIA 38-087066/CBS
21	26	29	7	**MAMA KNOWS** R.HALL, R.BYRNE (T.MENZIES, T.HASELDEN)	SHENANDOAH COLUMBIA 38-08042/CBS
22	27	33	5	**HOLD ME** H.SHEDD (K.T.OSLIN)	◆K.T.OSLIN RCA 8725-7
23	28	36	6	**WE MUST BE DOIN' SOMETHIN' RIGHT** R.LANDIS (E.RABBITT, R.NIELSEN)	EDDIE RABBITT RCA 8716-7

EXAMPLE

Darlene   What song was Number 1 last week?

Time for Entire Drill

Start

Finish

Answer

1. _____

2. _____

3. _____

4. _____

5. _____

6. _____

7. _____

8. _____

9. _____

10. _____

Question

1. What song was Number 2 this week?

2. Who sang the Number 10 song this week?

3. Who sang "Spanish Eyes"?

4. What is the newest song on the chart?

5. Where is Barbara Mandrell's song this week?

6. What label is "A Tender Lie" on?

7. Who produced "Blue to the Bone"?

8. Who wrote "I'll Leave This World Loving You"?

9. What song did B. Maher produce?

10. Where was "I Know How He Feels" two weeks ago?

Time for Each Item

1. _____ seconds

2. _____ seconds

3. _____ seconds

4. _____ seconds

5. _____ seconds

6. _____ seconds

7. _____ seconds

8. _____ seconds

9. _____ seconds

10. _____ seconds

ANSWER KEY: PAGE 138

Number Correct [   ]   Scanning Time [   ]

Billboard® HOT BLACK SINGLES™

THIS WEEK	LAST WEEK	2 WKS. AGO	WKS. ON CHART	Compiled from a national sample of retail stores and one-stop sales reports and radio playlists. TITLE PRODUCER (SONGWRITER)	ARTIST LABEL & NUMBER/DISTRIBUTING LABEL
				★★ No. 1 ★★	
(1)	2	5	8	**GIVING YOU THE BEST THAT I GOT** 1 week at No. One M.POWELL (A.BAKER, S.SCARBOROUGH, R.HOLLAND)	◆ANITA BAKER (C) ELEKTRA 7-69371
2	1	2	9	**ANY LOVE** L.VANDROSS, M.MILLER (L.VANDROSS, M.MILLER)	◆LUTHER VANDROSS (T) (C) EPIC 34-08047/E.P.A.
(3)	5	7	9	**THANKS FOR MY CHILD** FULL FORCE (FULL FORCE)	◆CHERYL "PEPSII" RILEY (T) (C) COLUMBIA 38-07996
4	7	8	9	**RESCUE ME** K.WEST, AL B.SURE! (AL B.SURE!, K.WEST)	◆AL B. SURE! (T) (C) WARNER BROS. 7-27762
5	3	4	11	**DON'T ROCK THE BOAT** MIDNIGHT STAR (B.SIMMONS)	◆MIDNIGHT STAR FEAT. ECSTACY OF WHODINI (T) (C) SOLAR 70027/CAPITOL
6	8	9	11	**MY GIRLY** READY FOR THE WORLD (M.RILEY, G.VALENTINE)	◆READY FOR THE WORLD (T) MCA 53337
(7)	12	17	8	**MY EYES DON'T CRY** S.WONDER (S.WONDER)	STEVIE WONDER (T) (C) MOTOWN 1946
8	10	16	10	**I CAN'T WAIT** G. DUKE (SKYLARK)	◆DENIECE WILLIAMS (T) COLUMBIA 38-08014
(9)	14	19	9	**MY HEART** C.BOOKER (C.BOOKER)	◆TROOP (T) (C) ATLANTIC 89023
10	11	15	10	**(IT'S JUST) THE WAY THAT YOU LOVE ME** O.LEIBER (O.LEIBER)	◆PAULA ABDUL (T) (C) VIRGIN 7-99282
(11)	17	23	7	**HEY LOVER** P.LAURENCE, D.SHEPHARD (S.MOORE, K.WASHINGTON)	FREDDIE JACKSON (T) (C) CAPITOL 44208
12	9	13	10	**DANCE LITTLE SISTER** M.WARE, T.T.D'ARBY (T.T.D'ARBY)	◆TERENCE TRENT D'ARBY (T) (C) (CD) COLUMBIA 38-08023
(13)	16	21	10	**GONNA GET OVER YOU** H.KING, CHAD (K.GREEN, K.GREEN, M.GREEN)	◆SWEET OBSESSION (T) EPIC 34 -07989/E.P.A.
14	6	1	13	**THE WAY YOU LOVE ME** L.A., BABYFACE (BABYFACE, L.A.REID, D.SIMMONS)	◆KARYN WHITE (T) WARNER BROS. 7-27773
(15)	20	26	6	**YOU MAKE ME WORK** L.BLACKMON (L.BLACKMON)	◆CAMEO (T) (C) (CD) ATLANTA ARTISTS 870 587-7/POLYGRAM
16	4	3	11	**YOU'RE NOT MY KIND OF GIRL** J.JAM, T.LEWIS (J.HARRIS III, T.LEWIS)	◆NEW EDITION (C) MCA 53405
(17)	19	24	8	**I MISSED** D.CONLEY, D.TOWNSEND, B.JACKSON (D.CONLEY, B.JACKSON, E.COLLINS)	SURFACE COLUMBIA 38-08018
(18)	22	29	8	**DIAL MY HEART** L.A., BABYFACE (L.A.REID, BABYFACE, D.SIMMONS)	◆THE BOYS (T) MOTOWN 53301
(19)	25	30	6	**EVERYTHING I MISS AT HOME** J.JAM, T.LEWIS (J.HARRIS III, T.LEWIS)	◆CHERRELLE (C) TABU 4-08052/E.P.A.
(20)	21	27	9	**CALLING THE LAW** REDDINGS (REDDINGS, AUTOFRAT)	◆THE REDDINGS (T) (C) POLYDOR 887 681-7/POLYGRAM

EXAMPLE

Anita Baker

What artist had the Number 1 song this week?

Time for Entire Drill

Start

Finish

Answer

1. _____

2. _____

3. _____

4. _____

5. _____

6. _____

7. _____

8. _____

9. _____

10. _____

Question

1. What song is Number 9 this week?

2. Who sang "My Eyes Don't Cry"?

3. Where was "Hey Lover" last week?

4. Who produced Karyn White?

5. Where is Cherrelle's record this week?

6. What label distributes "I Can't Wait"?

7. What was the top song last week?

8. What song did C. Booker write?

9. What song dropped in the charts the most this week?

10. What song has been on the chart the longest?

Time for Each Item

1. _____ seconds

2. _____ seconds

3. _____ seconds

4. _____ seconds

5. _____ seconds

6. _____ seconds

7. _____ seconds

8. _____ seconds

9. _____ seconds

10. _____ seconds

ANSWER KEY: PAGE 138

Number Correct [   ]   Scanning Time [   ]

Scanning Statistical Tables

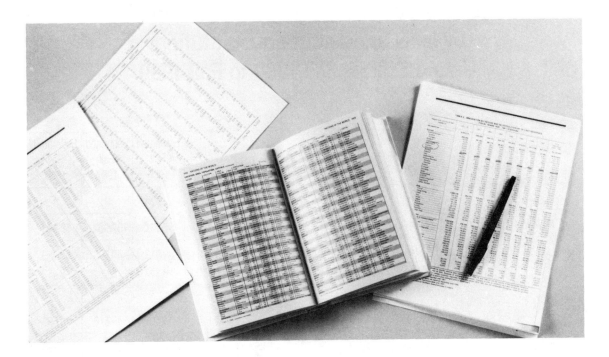

Reading a table is a useful and demanding skill. Few people ever read the whole thing. Usually a person will (1) read to find out how the table is arranged and (2) scan to find the desired information.

The following table is complex, but certainly not more complex than you will be called upon to read in many fields of science and social studies. Tables like this one appear in the fields of sociology, economics, education, and modern history.

Spend a few minutes getting acquainted with the table. Read the title, the column headings at the top of the chart, and the headings of the rows going across the page. This table, like many others, gives amounts in thousands. That means that the last three digits of the number are missing. If the table lists 58,414 for the number of students in all levels in fall 1980, this should be understood as 58,414,000.

Learning how to locate information in a statistical table now can save you time in the future. The following exercise will help you become familiar with tables while giving you scanning practice.

Directions: Take a few minutes to become familiar with the statistical table on page 116. Then read the questions and scan for the answers. Record your answers in the blanks provided. Study the example first.

As you do the exercise, scan for the answers as quickly as you can without sacrificing accuracy. When you have completed all 16 questions, turn to the answer key on page 139 and correct your answers.

For this exercise it is suggested that you take two timings to increase your skill at scanning quickly. Keep track of the time it takes you to complete all 16 questions. Record this time in the space provided.

Then go back and repeat the exercise to see if you can improve on your first timing. A second page of questions, identical to the first, has been provided on page 118. Keep track of how long it takes you to complete the exercise a second time and record your time in the space provided. Compare this timing with your first. Correct this second set of answers using the answer key on page 139.

Always strive for 100 percent accuracy. Scanning at a high rate of speed is useful only if you find the correct information. ▶

Enrollment in educational institutions, by level and control of institution: United States, Fall 1980 to Fall 1990

[in thousands]

Level of instruction and type of control	Fall 1980	Fall 1982	Fall 1983	Fall 1984	Fall 1985	Estimated Fall 1986	Estimated Fall 1987	Estimated Fall 1990
1	2	3	4	5	6	7	8	9
All levels	**58,414**	**57,678**	**57,532**	**57,235**	**57,360**	**57,710**	**57,984**	**58,911**
Public	50,444	49,348	49,035	48,770	48,992	49,312	49,503	50,459
Private	7,971	8,330	8,497	8,465	8,368	8,397	8,481	8,452
Elementary and secondary education	46,318	45,252	45,067	44,993	45,113	45,312	45,616	46,598
Public	40,987	39,652	39,352	39,293	39,513	39,712	39,916	40,898
Private	5,331	5,600	5,715	5,700	5,600	5,600	5,700	5,700
Grades K-8	31,666	31,356	31,312	31,218	31,347	31,655	32,228	34,128
Public	27,674	27,156	26,997	26,918	27,047	27,355	27,828	29,628
Private	3,992	4,200	4,315	4,300	4,300	4,300	4,400	4,500
Grades 9-12	14,652	13,896	13,755	13,775	13,767	13,657	13,388	12,470
Public	13,313	12,496	12,355	12,375	12,467	12,357	12,088	11,270
Private	1,339	1,400	1,400	1,400	1,300	1,300	1,300	1,200
Higher education	12,097	12,426	12,465	12,242	12,247	12,398	12,368	12,313
Public	9,457	9,696	9,683	9,477	9,479	9,600	9,587	9,561
Undergraduate	8,442	8,713	8,697	8,493	8,477	8,577	8,546	8,489
First-professional	114	113	113	114	112	114	115	117
Graduate	901	870	872	870	890	909	926	955
Private	2,640	2,730	2,782	2,765	2,768	2,797	2,781	2,752
Undergraduate	2,033	2,112	2,149	2,125	2,120	2,147	2,123	2,097
First-professional	163	165	165	165	162	163	168	165
Graduate	443	453	468	475	486	487	490	490

EXAMPLE

_58,414,000_   How many students were in all levels in fall 1980?

Time for Entire Drill

Start

Finish

Answer

Question

Time for Each Item

1. _____

1. How many students were in all levels in fall 1985?

1. _____ seconds

2. _____

2. How many students were estimated to be in all levels in fall 1990?

2. _____ seconds

3. _____

3. How many students were in Higher Education in fall 1982?

3. _____ seconds

4. _____

4. How many students were in grades 9–12 (public and private) in fall 1982?

4. _____ seconds

5. _____

5. What was the total number of students in K–8 in Fall 1984?

5. _____ seconds

6. _____

6. What was the total number of students in K–8 estimated for fall 1990?

6. _____ seconds

7. _____

7. How many students were in grades K–8 private only in fall 1985?

7. _____ seconds

8. _____

8. How many students were in public higher education in fall 1984?

8. _____ seconds

9. _____

9. How many students were in private graduate education in fall 1985?

9. _____ seconds

10. _____

10. How many students were estimated to be in public undergraduate education in fall 1987?

10. _____ seconds

11. _____

11. How many students were in all levels of private education in fall 1985?

11. _____ seconds

12. _____

12. How many students were estimated to be in grades 9–12 in public schools in fall 1990?

12. _____ seconds

13. _____

13. How many students are in public schools grades K–8 in fall 1985?

13. _____ seconds

14. _____

14. How many students are undergraduates in public institutions in fall 1982?

14. _____ seconds

15. _____

15. How many students were in all levels in fall 1982?

15. _____ seconds

16. _____

16. What was the total number of students in higher education in fall 1984?

16. _____ seconds

ANSWER KEY: PAGE 139

Number Correct

Scanning Time

Enrollment in educational institutions, by level and control of institution: United States, Fall 1980 to Fall 1990

[in thousands]

Level of instruction and type of control	Fall 1980	Fall 1982	Fall 1983	Fall 1984	Fall 1985	Estimated Fall 1986	Estimated Fall 1987	Estimated Fall 1990
1	2	3	4	5	6	7	8	9
All levels	**58,414**	**57,678**	**57,532**	**57,235**	**57,360**	**57,710**	**57,984**	**58,911**
Public	50,444	49,348	49,035	48,770	48,992	49,312	49,503	50,459
Private	7,971	8,330	8,497	8,465	8,368	8,397	8,481	8,452
Elementary and secondary education	46,318	45,252	45,067	44,993	45,113	45,312	45,616	46,598
Public	40,987	39,652	39,352	39,293	39,513	39,712	39,916	40,898
Private	5,331	5,600	5,715	5,700	5,600	5,600	5,700	5,700
Grades K-8	31,666	31,356	31,312	31,218	31,347	31,655	32,228	34,128
Public	27,674	27,156	26,997	26,918	27,047	27,355	27,828	29,628
Private	3,992	4,200	4,315	4,300	4,300	4,300	4,400	4,500
Grades 9-12	14,652	13,896	13,755	13,775	13,767	13,657	13,388	12,470
Public	13,313	12,496	12,355	12,375	12,467	12,357	12,088	11,270
Private	1,339	1,400	1,400	1,400	1,300	1,300	1,300	1,200
Higher education	12,097	12,426	12,465	12,242	12,247	12,398	12,368	12,313
Public	9,457	9,696	9,683	9,477	9,479	9,600	9,587	9,561
Undergraduate	8,442	8,713	8,697	8,493	8,477	8,577	8,546	8,489
First-professional	114	113	113	114	112	114	115	117
Graduate	901	870	872	870	890	909	926	955
Private	2,640	2,730	2,782	2,765	2,768	2,797	2,781	2,752
Undergraduate	2,033	2,112	2,149	2,125	2,120	2,147	2,123	2,097
First-professional	163	165	165	165	162	163	168	165
Graduate	443	453	468	475	486	487	490	490

EXAMPLE

_58,414,000_   How many students were in all levels in fall 1980?

Time for Entire Drill

Start

Finish

Answer

1. _____
2. _____
3. _____
4. _____
5. _____
6. _____
7. _____
8. _____
9. _____
10. _____
11. _____
12. _____
13. _____
14. _____
15. _____
16. _____

Question

1. How many students were in all levels in fall 1985?
2. How many students were estimated to be in all levels in fall 1990?
3. How many students were in Higher Education in fall 1982?
4. How many students were in grades 9–12 (public and private) in fall 1982?
5. What was the total number of students in K–8 in Fall 1984?
6. What was the total number of students in K–8 estimated for fall 1990?
7. How many students were in grades K–8 private only in fall 1985?
8. How many students were in public higher education in fall 1984?
9. How many students were in private graduate education in fall 1985?
10. How many students were estimated to be in public undergraduate education in fall 1987?
11. How many students were in all levels of private education in fall 1985?
12. How many students were estimated to be in grades 9–12 in public schools in fall 1990?
13. How many students are in public schools grades K–8 in fall 1985?
14. How many students are undergraduates in public institutions in fall 1982?
15. How many students were in all levels in fall 1982?
16. What was the total number of students in higher education in fall 1984?

Time for Each Item

1. _____ seconds
2. _____ seconds
3. _____ seconds
4. _____ seconds
5. _____ seconds
6. _____ seconds
7. _____ seconds
8. _____ seconds
9. _____ seconds
10. _____ seconds
11. _____ seconds
12. _____ seconds
13. _____ seconds
14. _____ seconds
15. _____ seconds
16. _____ seconds

ANSWER KEY: PAGE 139

Number Correct _____   Scanning Time _____

Scanning Newspaper Articles

Not all scanning is done with alphabetized lists of words or numerical tables. Often you need to locate just one specific bit of information from a whole page of material. Scanning for specific facts in an article or passage is a very useful skill to develop.

The following exercises will give you a chance to practice scanning a newspaper article. Begin by taking a few minutes to become familiar with the arrangement of information. Read the title, the subheads, and the first and last paragraphs. Next, read the first question and decide what clue words will help you locate the section of the article you need. You are now ready to scan for the answer.

Note that although one newspaper article is used as an example, it is divided into Article A and Article B, and each part is timed separately.

Speed is essential; do not try to *read* sentences. Merely scan the columns until you locate a section which promises to contain the information you need. Once the appropriate area has been found, begin to read bits of sentences more carefully until you find the correct answer.

Strive for 100 percent accuracy. Since your objective is to locate the exact spot in the article where the answer is located, there is no excuse for not getting accurate answers for every question.

Don't confuse this with a skimming exercise in which you are seeking an overall understanding of the main ideas of the entire passage. Your objective in scanning is to locate a specific bit of information.

Although the exercises each ask five questions, do not try to save time by reading the entire articles first. There will be many times when you will want to scan a newspaper article or encyclopedia quickly to locate only one or two specific bits of information. Hence, treat each question as if it were the only one you want to answer.

Directions: When scanning the following newspaper articles, strive for speed and accuracy. Timing yourself as you do the entire exercise may help to increase your speed.

Begin by taking a few minutes to become familiar with the arrangement of information in the articles. Then make a note of the time and begin to read the first question. Do not read more than one question before beginning to scan for the information. When you have located the answer, write it in the blank provided and go on to the next question. Study the example first.

Make a note of your finishing time when you have written your last answer. Figure your total time and record it in the space provided. Compare your time with that of other students in your class.

Be certain that your answers are correct. There is no reason why they shouldn't be accurate since every answer can be located in the article. Your objective should be to find the information you need quickly without reading more than is absolutely necessary. When finished, correct your answers using the answer key on page 139. ▶

THE NEW YORK TIMES

The Wolf Is Getting a Better Image with Help of a Biologist

ELY, Minn. — A crimson pool of blood lay frozen in the snow. Ravens pecked at the last shreds of what had been a deer.

"There they are!" David Mech, wolf biologist, shouted over the roar of a Cessna 180 circling tightly above the frozen lake as he pointed down at the shore. "The wolves!"

About a hundred yards from the kill in the middle of the lake, six timber wolves rested drowsily after the kill in the cold, bright sun. One jumped up to watch the little plane as it banked sharply.

Dr. L. David Mech, who has studied wolves for 18 years and is widely acknowledged as this country's leading expert on wolf behavior, marked down on a tracking form the location of the wolves, how many there were and what they were doing. Then he directed the pilot to head southwest toward the place where another wolf pack had last been seen.

Through such aerial observations, a technique he helped develop, Dr. Mech has gathered much of the evidence that has debunked many of man's oldest myths about the wolf.

Once widely hated and persecuted as a dangerous predator, the wolf today, thanks largely to Dr. Mech's research, is coming to be regarded as an ecologically important member of its wilderness habitats and as an animal with a complex and fascinating society. Once feared as dangerous to people, the wolf is now known not only as friendly and sociable within its pack, but as no threat to man. There is no documented instance of a free-living wolf attacking a person in North America.

Dr. Mech (pronounced Meech), now 40 years old, began his wolf research in 1959 as a graduate student while observing the two dozen wolves of Isle Royale National Park in Lake Superior. Today, employed by the Endangered Wildlife Research Program of the United States Fish and Wildlife Service, he is in charge of a wide-ranging, long-term study of the relatively stable population of 1,000 to 1,200 wolves in northern Minnesota. These animals are the last substantial population of wolves in the United States outside of Alaska.

The greatest concentration of these wolves is in the Superior National Forest near here in the extreme northeastern corner of the state, and the dead of winter, when the beasts can be spotted against the snow, is the best time for studying them.

As the little plane headed toward the next wolf pack sighting, Dr. Mech put his headphones back on and listened intently for a clicking signal picked up by antennas mounted on the plane's wing struts.

One of the wolves in the pack, like one in the pack sighted near its kill, was wearing a tiny, battery-powered transmitter on a collar around its neck. The signal from this constantly operating device picked up by the antennas on the plane guides Dr. Mech to the wolves.

Over the years Dr. Mech and his assistants, most of them graduate students in wildlife biology at the University of Minnesota, have trapped and radio-tagged about 140 wolves in the Superior National Forest area.

After being captured in a modified leg-hold trap, the wolves are immobilized with drugs, weighed, and identified by sex. Blood samples are taken. Ear tags are clipped on and the collar is fitted. As the drugs wear off, the wolf, transmitting on its own frequency, runs off to rejoin its pack. Because wolf packs are stable social units, the signal from a single radio collar can lead Dr. Mech or his students to the entire pack.

Because the antennas are highly directional, picking up signals from either the left or right side of the plane, depending on which antenna is used, Dr. Mech can tell where the transmitting wolf is in relationship to the plane. Dr. Mech can switch from one antenna to the other. When the signal is equally strong from the two antennas, the plane is headed directly for the wolves.

Twenty-four of the 140 radio collars are still working, the others either have stopped operating (usually after a year or so) or the wolves have been killed (wolves that venture too near human beings risk being shot or trapped). The 24 tagged animals represent nine packs, one newly formed pair that may breed to establish a new pack, and four lone wolves, animals who have left their original packs to wander alone and sometimes find a mate and a vacant "territory" in which they can establish a new pack.

Minutes after leaving the pack with the deer kill, Dr. Mech signaled the pilot to circle above a forested ridge.

"They're down there," Dr. Mech shouted. "Can't see 'em. They're probably under the trees."

After logging their position and that of some other packs, Dr. Mech headed back to the airport. Every day during winter and at least weekly during the summer Dr. Mech or his students go up in planes to find the collared wolves. One pack has been tracked for six years.

When the locations for a given wolf pack are plotted on a map, almost all fall within a tightly circumscribed territory abutting the territories of other wolf packs and almost never overlapping them. One pack, for example, has fluctuated from two to nine members over the years, but has always maintained the same territorial boundaries with its neighboring packs. On a larger scale, wolf densities usually are about one for every 10 square miles.

Continued on page 124

EXAMPLE

18 years

For how long has Dr. David Mech studied wolves?

The answer is located at the beginning of the fourth paragraph in Article A.

Time for Article A

Start

Finish

Answer

Question

1. _____

1. How many wolves have Dr. Mech and his assistants trapped and tagged?

2. _____

2. In North America has an attack on humans by a wolf ever been documented?

3. _____

3. Do wolf pack territories usually overlap?

4. _____

4. How many wolves is Dr. Mech in charge of studying in northern Minnesota?

5. _____

5. What kind of identification is attached to a wolf at the same time the radio collars are fitted?

ANSWER KEY: PAGE 139

Number Correct

Scanning Time

Continued from page 122

Wolves mark the boundaries with urine and, even when chasing prey, seldom enter alien territory. When they do, they risk attack from the resident pack.

Back at the log cabin on a Forest Service compound near Ely that serves as the wolf study's field station, Dr. Mech and half a dozen students come and go throughout the day, drying out soaked gloves, pouring hot coffee, calibrating radio receivers, exchanging information on the day's sightings. In the refrigerator, vials of wolf blood share space with bottles of beer. Several of the students track wolves from the air and others manage projects on deer, lynxes, moose, snowshoe hares, ravens, and other local fauna. Many of these animals are also wearing radio collars.

By studying both wolves and their prey, Dr. Mech and his students hope to discover and understand those elements of their behavior that have evolved as ways of coping with the other species. Anatomical adaptations for attack and defense are well known but behavioral adaptations are not.

Biologists have long known that wolves have developed certain ways of hunting that maximize their chances of killing deer. Presumably deer, who heretofore have not been intensively studied as one-half of a predator-prey relationship, have evolved defensive behaviors as well.

One deer behavior that is under study is the congregating of deer in open meadows, or deer yards, in the winter. In spring and winter deer are dispersed through the forest. Why do deer shift back and forth between two different systems of social organization?

Somehow, Dr. Mech suspects, the deer's slower metabolism in winter, the difficulty of moving in snow and the fact that fawns have grown more independent since their birth make "yarding" a better way to defend against wolves in winter but a poorer way in summer. A four-year study of deer behavior is planned in an attempt to explain this phenomenon.

One recent morning a student reported that wolf No. 2407 and its pack were found well out of their territory. Dr. Mech checked the location on a map. "That's interesting," he remarked. "Those sons of guns, they're trespassing, really striking out on their own." From the map it appeared that they would have had to cross two roads to reach their present location from where they had been the day before.

Later in the day, after a futile attempt to find a radio-collared wolf that someone reported seeing on a road with a trap on its foot, Dr. Mech drove the snow-covered roads that the "trespassing" wolves had crossed to look for scent marks. When wolves cross a road or other physical boundary, they mark the junction with urine. He wanted to collect urine samples frozen into the snow for biochemical analysis but a snowplow had recently obliterated the marks.

Some Still Hunt Wolves

The biologists' interactions with the human population in and around Ely have proven both rewarding and frustrating.

Dr. Mech said that although most townspeople were sympathetic to the wolf research and favored the species' protection, a few retained the older antipathy. There is a vigilante group that kills wolves whenever possible and puts the carcasses on other people's doorsteps with notes arguing that wolves destroy deer that should be protected for hunters.

Although wolf hunting and trapping have been illegal in Minnesota since 1965, it continues. Whenever one of the collared wolves is killed, however, some sympathetic trappers notify Dr. Mech by leaving anonymous notes at a local bar.

Because some of Dr. Mech's colleagues study deer, some townspeople are puzzled that scientists who specialize in species that are seen as "natural enemies" can be friends.

"We have a ways to go in changing people's attitudes about these animals," Dr. Mech said.

Dr. Mech says he likes to get into the field as often as possible but noted that he had a desk job with the Fish and Wildlife Service in St. Paul. There, with access to libraries and laboratories, he writes scientific papers on wolf behavior, consults with scientists and conservationists around the world. Last year he spent a month in India training biologists there in radio tracking. He also develops strategies for protecting wolves.

For example, Dr. Mech was heavily involved in the 1974 effort to relocate four Minnesota wolves in Michigan's Upper Peninsula. Within eight months after the wolves were released, all four, two males and two females, had been killed by human beings. Two were shot; one was trapped and then shot; one was hit by a car.

Animals Can Be Relocated

The experiment did establish that relocated wolves could establish themselves in a new territory and survive. "The problem," Dr. Mech said, "is the human population. Next time we would want to do a more intensive public education effort."

Dr. Mech is a member of the Eastern Timber Wolf Recovery Team appointed by the Fish and Wildlife Service to devise a program for the protection and reestablishment of wolf populations. The group has suggested that wolves be reintroduced to wilderness areas in Michigan, Wisconsin, New York State's Adirondacks, Maine, and the Great Smoky Mountain National Park.

Dr. Mech has found that wolves can double their numbers every year. However, they do not if the area is already full and each pack's territory abuts others on all sides. Lone wolves, unable to establish a territory near their place of origin, disperse to a less desirable habitat and, in many cases, are killed by people.

Thus, Dr. Mech has found, wolf hunting or trapping can continue at a substantial rate on the fringes of prime wolf country without lowering the average wolf population.

In Minnesota, for example, the Wolf Recovery Team has recommended that controlled wolf killing be permitted in a buffer zone around the wolf's 10,000-square-mile prime range, which would remain totally protected. Limited wolf hunting or trapping, the group believes, is necessary to minimize the loss of livestock to wolves and to increase the base of local citizen support for conservation, without which wolves might not survive at all.

Answer   **Question**

6. _____   6. What two words best describe the
                                    interactions between the biologists and the
                                    human population in Ely?

7. _____   7. How often can the wolf population double
                                    under ideal conditions?

8. _____   8. In which season is "yarding" a better way
                                    for deer to defend themselves?

9. _____   9. In what kind of building is the field
                                    station located?

10. _____   10. How long has wolf hunting been illegal
                                     in Minnesota?

ANSWER KEY: PAGE 139		
Number Correct		Scanning Time

Scanning Documents

A set of laws or rules is seldom read from beginning to end. However, from time to time it becomes necessary to refer to specific parts of such documents. Scanning provides the most efficient means for locating the information you need.

Take a moment to note the organization of the *United Nations Declaration of Human Rights* used in these two exercises. The material is organized in short, numbered passages called *articles*. As you scan for the required information, strive for speed plus accuracy.

Note that although one document is used as an example, it is divided into Part A and Part B, and each part is timed separately.

The *Declaration of Human Rights* is an interesting document. You will discover that the United States, as well as many other countries, are fortunate to have most of the rights listed. In some countries, however, they are woefully lacking. You may find yourself becoming interested in reading this document at length. If so, be sure to continue using your scanning technique until *all* of the questions have been answered. *After* you have completed the exercises, go back and read the sections which interest you.

Directions: Begin by taking a few minutes to look at the arrangement of the information. Then make a note of the time and begin to read the first question. Do not read the whole declaration. Scan the first statement or phrase of each article to find out what it is about, then move quickly on to the next until you locate the exact information you need.

Sometimes the exact wording will be at the beginning of the article and sometimes toward the end. In some instances, however, only part of the phrase is there, or the exact wording is separated by other words. Thus, when you come upon an article which seems to contain the information you are seeking, read it carefully to find the answer.

Don't be too quick to accept an article that is too general. For example, the third article is about liberty. This could apply to a good many rights, but it is too general. You are scanning for articles which apply specifically to the topic for which you are searching. Your goal is 100 percent accuracy.

Do one question at a time. When you have located an answer, record the number of the article on the line provided. Then go on to the next question. Study the example first.

Make a note of your finishing time when you have written your last answer. Figure your total time and record it in the space provided. Compare your time with that of other students in your class. When finished, correct your answers using the answer key on page 139. ▶

THE UNIVERSAL DECLARATION OF HUMAN RIGHTS

Article 1 All human beings are born free and equal in dignity and rights. They are endowed with reason and conscience and should act toward one another in a spirit of brotherhood.

Article 2 Everyone is entitled to all the rights and freedoms set forth in this Declaration, without distinction of any kind, such as race, color, sex, language, religion, political, or other opinion, national or social origin, property, birth, or other status.
　　Furthermore, no distinction shall be made on the basis of the political, jurisdictional, or international status of the country or territory to which a person belongs, whether it be independent, trust, non-self-governing, or under any other limitation of sovereignty.

Article 3 Everyone has the right to life, liberty, and the security of person.

Article 4 No one shall be held in slavery or servitude; slavery and the slave trade shall be prohibited in all their forms.

Article 5 No one shall be subjected to torture or to cruel, inhuman, or degrading treatment or punishment.

Article 6 Everyone has the right to recognition everywhere as a person before the law.

Article 7 All are equal before the law and are entitled without any discrimination to equal protection of the law. All are entitled to equal protection against any discrimination in violation of this Declaration and against any incitement to such discrimination.

Article 8 Everyone has the right to an effective remedy by the competent national tribunals for acts violating the fundamental rights granted him or her by the constitution or by law.

Article 9 No one shall be subjected to arbitrary arrest, detention, or exile.

Article 10 Everyone is entitled in full equality to a fair and public hearing by an independent and impartial tribunal, in the determination of his or her rights and obligations and of any criminal charge against him or her.

Article 11 1. Everyone charged with a penal offense has the right to be presumed innocent until proved guilty according to law in a public trial at which he or she has had all the guarantees necessary for his or her defense.
2. No one shall be held guilty of any penal offense on account of any act or omission which did not constitute a penal offense, under national or international law, at the time when it was committed. Nor shall a heavier penalty be imposed than the one that was applicable at the time the penal offense was committed.

Article 12 No one shall be subjected to arbitrary interference with his or her privacy, family, home, or correspondence, nor to attacks upon his or her honor and reputation. Everyone has the right to the protection of the law against such interference or attacks.

Article 13 1. Everyone has the right to freedom of movement and residence within the borders of each State.
2. Everyone has the right to leave any country including his or her own, and to return to his or her country.

Article 14 1. Everyone has the right to seek and to enjoy in other countries asylum from persecution.
2. This right may not be invoked in the case of prosecutions genuinely arising from nonpolitical crimes or from acts contrary to the purposes and principles of the United Nations.

Article 15 1. Everyone has the right to a nationality.
2. No one shall be arbitrarily deprived of his or her nationality.

Article 16 1. Men and women of full age, without any limitation due to race, nationality, or religion, have the right to marry and to found a family. They are entitled to equal rights as to marriage, during marriage, and at its dissolution.
2. Marriage shall be entered into only with the free and full consent of the intending spouses.
3. The family is the natural and fundamental group unit of society and is entitled to protection by society and the State.

Continued on page 130

EXAMPLE

life, liberty, and security of person   Article ___3___

Time for Part A

Start [ ]

Finish [ ]

Item

1. no one held in slavery

2. right to marry

3. no one subject to arbitrary arrest

4. right to seek asylum in other countries

5. everyone innocent until proved guilty

6. no one tortured

7. right to return to one's own country

8. freedom of movement between states

9. right to a nationality

10. equal before the law and entitled to equal protection of the law

Answer

1. Article _____

2. Article _____

3. Article _____

4. Article _____

5. Article _____

6. Article _____

7. Article _____

8. Article _____

9. Article _____

10. Article _____

ANSWER KEY: PAGE 139

Number Correct [ ]   Scanning Time [ ]

THE UNIVERSAL DECLARATION OF HUMAN RIGHTS

Continued from page 128

Article 17 1. Everyone has the right to own property alone as well as in association with others.
2. No one shall be arbitrarily deprived of his or her property.

Article 18 Everyone has the right to freedom of thought, conscience, and religion; this right includes freedom to change his or her religion or belief, the freedom, either alone or in community with others and in public or private, to manifest his or her religion or belief in teaching, practice, worship, and observance.

Article 19 Everyone has the right to freedom of opinion and expression; this right includes freedom to hold opinions without interference and to seek, receive, and impart information and ideas through any media and regardless of frontiers.

Article 20 1. Everyone has the right to freedom of peaceful assembly and association.
2. No one may be compelled to belong to an association.

Article 21 1. Everyone has the right to take part in the government of his or her country, directly or through freely chosen representatives.
2. Everyone has the right of equal access to public service in his or her country.
3. The will of the people shall be the basis of the authority of government; this will shall be expressed in periodic and genuine elections which shall be by universal and equal suffrage and shall be held by secret vote or by equivalent free voting procedures.

Article 22 Everyone, as a member of society, has the right to social security and is entitled to realization, through national effort and international cooperation and in accordance with the organization and resources of each State, of the economic, social, and cultural rights indispensable for his or her dignity and the free development of his or her personality.

Article 23 1. Everyone has the right to work, to free choice of employment, to just and favorable conditions of work, and to protection against unemployment.
2. Everyone, without any discrimination, has the right to equal pay for equal work.
3. Everyone who works has the right to just and favorable remuneration ensuring for himself or herself and his or her family an existence worthy of human dignity, and supplemented, if necessary, by other means of social protection.
4. Everyone has the right to form and to join trade unions for the protection of his or her interests.

Article 24 Everyone has the right to rest and leisure, including reasonable limitation of working hours and periodic holidays with pay.

Article 25 1. Everyone has the right to a standard of living adequate for the health and well-being of himself or herself and of his or her family, including food, clothing, housing, and medical care and necessary social services, and the right to security in the event of unemployment, sickness, disability, widowhood, old age, or other lack of livelihood in circumstances beyond his control.
2. Motherhood and childhood are entitled to special care and assistance. All children, whether born in or out of wedlock, shall enjoy the same social protection.

Article 26 1. Everyone has the right to education. Education shall be free, at least in the elementary and fundamental stages. Elementary education shall be compulsory. Technical and professional education shall be made generally available and higher education shall be equally accessible to all on the basis of merit.
2. Education shall be directed to the full development of the human personality and to the strengthening of respect for human rights and fundamental freedoms. It shall promote understanding, tolerance, and friendship among all nations, racial, or religious groups, and shall further the activities of the United Nations for the maintenance of peace.
3. Parents have a prior right to choose the kind of education that shall be given to their children.

Article 27 1. Everyone has the right freely to participate in the cultural life of the community, to enjoy the arts, and to share in scientific advancement and its benefits.
2. Everyone has the right to the protection of the moral and material interests resulting from any scientific, literary, or artistic production of which he or she is the author.

This document is a shortened version of the Universal Declaration of Human Rights adopted by the United Nations General Assembly, December 10, 1948.

Time for Part B	
Start	
Finish	

Item

11. free choice of employment

12. right of parents to choose the kind of education for their children

13. right to own property

14. right to rest and leisure

15. right to participate in cultural life of the community

16. right to join a trade union

17. right to peaceful assembly

18. right to free elementary education

19. right to take part in government

20. right to freedom of religion

Answer

11. Article _____

12. Article _____

13. Article _____

14. Article _____

15. Article _____

16. Article _____

17. Article _____

18. Article _____

19. Article _____

20. Article _____

ANSWER KEY: PAGE 139

Number Correct [ ]　　Scanning Time [ ]

Scanning Reference Materials

As a student, you are often asked to supplement your textbooks with a variety of resource material. A wide range of reference works are available in libraries. Supplementary material may take the form of encyclopedias, government publications, journals and periodicals, textbooks other than your basic text for the course, and pamphlets from many sources.

Whatever the resource, often only a section of it will contain material for your assignment. The task of wading through such material can be overwhelming and time-consuming unless you are able to scan for the information you need.

The following exercise will help you improve your skill at scanning reference material. Using the scanning technique discussed in this text will enable you to uncover a wealth of material efficiently and accurately.

Directions: When scanning the following material, strive for speed and accuracy. Timing yourself as you do the entire exercise may help to increase your speed.

Begin by taking a few minutes to become familiar with the arrangement of the information in both passages. Then make a note of the time and begin to read the first question. When you have located the answer, write it in the blank provided and go on to the next question. Study the example first.

Make a note of your finishing time when you have written your last answer. Figure your total time and record it in the space provided. Compare your time with that of other students in your class.

Your goal should be 100 percent accuracy. Scanning at a high rate of speed is useful only if you find the exact information you need. When finished, correct your answers using the answer key on page 139. ▶

REFERENCE A: HISTORY

To properly understand the condition of things preceding the great war of the rebellion, we must glance backward through the history of the country to that memorable 30th of November, 1782. It was then that the independence of the United States of America was at last conceded by Great Britain.

At that time the population of the United States was about 2,500,000 free whites and some 500,000 black slaves. We had gained our independence of the Mother Country, but she had left fastened upon us the curse of slavery. Indeed, African slavery had already been implanted on the soil of Virginia before Plymouth Rock was pressed by the feet of the Pilgrim Fathers. Slavery had soon spread, with greater or less rapidity according to the surrounding adaptations of soil, production, and climate to every one of the thirteen colonies.

Slavery, thus, was recognized and acquiesced in by all as an existing and established institution. Yet there were many, both in the South and North, who looked upon it as an evil—an inherited evil—and were anxious to prevent the increase of that evil. Hence it was that even as far back as 1699 a controversy sprang up between the colonies and the home government upon the African slavery question—a controversy continuing with more or less vehemence down to the Declaration of Independence itself.

It was this conviction that slavery was not only an evil but a dangerous evil that induced Jefferson to embody in his original draft of that declaration a clause strongly condemnatory of the African slave trade. Later, this clause was omitted from the declaration solely, he tells us, "in complaisance to South Carolina and Georgia, who had never attempted to restrain the importation of slaves and who, on the contrary, still wished to continue it," as well as in deference to the sensitiveness of Northern people who, though having few slaves themselves, "had been pretty considerable carriers of them to others. . . ."

REFERENCE B: GEOGRAPHY

Geographically, France is a quadrilateral bounded, except to the northeast, by natural frontiers: to the west, the English Channel and the Atlantic; to the south, the Pyrenees and the Mediterranean; to the east, the Alps, the Jura, and the Rhine. Within these frontiers, plains traversed by rivers and verdant hill country surround the "Massif Central" that consists of high plateaux and extinct volcanoes.

The scenery is quite varied: imposing in the eternal snows of the Alps and the Pyrenees, fertile and harmonious where there are rivers, rough and picturesque on the Atlantic coast, and luxuriant and smiling on the shores of the deep blue Mediterranean. The climate varies considerably: fairly rough, though not bleak, in the north; mild, equable, and inclined to be rainy in the west; dryer in the east, with greater contrasts; and sunny and dry in the south.

France is a rich country. This is reflected in the mode of life of the people. The north and the center contain many important industries that are grouped round rich deposits of coal and iron ore. The whole country produces cereals, vegetables, fruit, and other agricultural produce in abundance. Vineyards dominate the scene on the sunny shores of the Mediterranean, in the Rhone Valley, in Burgundy, and in other climatically privileged parts of the country.

The French Republic has an area of 550.986 kilometers and a population of 42.9 million (not counting overseas territories). The population of Greater Paris is nearly 5 million. The rest of the country is poor in great cities; the fourth largest city in France—Toulouse—has a population of only 265,000. In spite of the continuous process of urbanization in the 20th century, most French people continue to live in villages or small provincial towns. Love of the native soil is one of the most pronounced and deeply rooted national characteristics of the French.

EXAMPLE

_500,000_

How many slaves were there in the U.S. at the time of independence?

Time for Entire Drill

Start

Finish

Answer

Question

REFERENCE A

1. _____

1. How many whites were there in the U.S. at the time of independence?

2. _____

2. Where was slavery first started (implanted) in the U.S.?

3. _____

3. Did Jefferson favor slavery?

4. _____

4. When did Britain concede independence?

5. _____

5. Did all 13 colonies have slaves?

REFERENCE B

6. _____

6. How big is France in area?

7. _____

7. What bounds France on the west?

8. _____

8. Name two valuable deposits mined in northern and central France.

9. _____

9. Which area is mild and rainy?

10. _____

10. What is the population of Greater Paris?

ANSWER KEY: PAGE 139

Number Correct

Scanning Time

Answer Key

Part 1: Skimming

1 Alexander Dolgun's Story

1. b	6. c
2. a	7. c
3. c	8. a
4. b	9. c
5. b	10. b

2 To Sir, with Love

1. b	6. c
2. c	7. a
3. b	8. c
4. c	9. a
5. a	10. c

3 Alive

1. b	6. c
2. a	7. b
3. b	8. a
4. c	9. b
5. b	10. b

4 Roots

1. a	6. c
2. a	7. a
3. c	8. a
4. c	9. c
5. b	10. a

5 Reincarnation and 13 Pairs of Socks

1. b	6. c
2. b	7. c
3. c	8. c
4. b	9. b
5. a	10. c

6 Sharks

1. a	6. b
2. c	7. b
3. c	8. c
4. b	9. a
5. c	10. c

7 My Early Life

1. c	6. b
2. b	7. c
3. c	8. b
4. b	9. a
5. a	10. b

8 Hour of Gold, Hour of Lead

1. a	6. b
2. b	7. a
3. c	8. c
4. c	9. c
5. a	10. b

9 Centennial

1. c	6. a
2. b	7. c
3. a	8. b
4. c	9. c
5. a	10. a

10 Body Language

1. c	6. c
2. b	7. c
3. b	8. a
4. a	9. c
5. b	10. c

Answer Key

Part 2: Scanning

1 Scanning Alphabetical Lists

1. justifiably
2. irritably
3. knavishly
4. lazily
5. jauntily
6. impurely
7. liberally
8. inauspiciously
9. insurmountably
10. irksomely
11. impatiently
12. incomprehensibly
13. joyfully
14. lawfully
15. immodestly
16. inconclusively
17. inexcusably
18. interchangeably
19. indiscreetly
20. inexpensively

2 Scanning Guide Words

PART A

1. 102
2. 96
3. 104
4. 108
5. 98
6. 102
7. 110
8. 94
9. 112
10. 100
11. 106
12. 111
13. 95
14. 107
15. 112
16. 109
17. 98
18. 114
19. 103
20. 99
21. 116
22. 114
23. 105
24. 96
25. 102
26. 105
27. 98
28. 95
29. 112
30. 116

PART B

1. 283
2. 287
3. 287
4. 290
5. 282
6. 294
7. 293
8. 301
9. 284
10. 297
11. 304
12. 292
13. 302
14. 302
15. 291
16. 295
17. 297
18. 292
19. 296
20. 299

3 Scanning Telephone Directories

1. 828-4662
2. 884-5245
3. 725-5234
4. 331-3331
5. 737-6424
6. 726-0733
7. 245-1279
8. 695-3110
9. 725-3030
10. 421-8387
11. 467-9812
12. 695-6516
13. 944-8017
14. 437-0897
15. 245-9496
16. 737-2271
17. 722-9896
18. 724-2184
19. 821-7891
20. 821-8499

4 Scanning Indexes

1. 278
2. 8
3. 102
4. 418
5. 248
6. 584
7. 339
8. 12
9. 80
10. 128
11. 351
12. 736
13. 226
14. 190
15. 808
16. 265
17. 595
18. 87
19. 308
20. 69
21. 339
22. 382
23. 574
24. 109
25. 124
26. 71
27. 542
28. 752
29. 793
30. 134

5 Scanning TV Listings

1. 2, 6, 7
2. LIF (Lifetime)
3. 7:00 or 8:00
4. a television show describing explorers from around the world
5. 18, 34, 52
6. 56
7. no
8. a drama
9. the Philippines
10. one hour
11. 7:00
12. Evert and Navratilova

6 Scanning Train Schedules

1. 174, 176
2. 174
3. 212
4. 4:10 P.M.
5. 8:25 P.M.
6. no
7. 4:45 P.M.
8. 166 miles
9. 1 day
10. 6 days
11. 4 hours, 15 minutes
12. 4 hours, 30 minutes
13. 11:05 A.M.
14. 10 minutes
15. 15 minutes

7 Scanning Best-Seller Lists

1. *The Queen of the Damned*
2. William Manchester
3. number 9
4. McGraw-Hill
5. the Billy-the-Kid legend
6. nonfiction
7. Kirk Douglas
8. 49
9. *One*
10. *The Sands of Time*
11. *A Brief History of Time*
12. $21.95
13. *Child Star* and *The Ragman's Son*
14. *Dragonsdawn*
15. *The 8-Week Cholesterol Cure*

8 Scanning Hit-Record Charts

PART A

1. "Bad Medicine"
2. number 12
3. "A Word in Spanish"
4. "Red Red Wine"
5. N. Diamond
6. Narada
7. "Groovy Kind of Love"
8. "I Don't Want Your Love"
9. The Beach Boys
10. number 22

PART B

1. "Que Sera"
2. MCA
3. "Cara Dura"
4. Charytin
5. "Es Un Alma en Pena"
6. "Ya No"
7. Luis Enrique
8. RCA
9. number 6
10. "Una Mujer Como Tu"

PART C

1. "New Shade of Blue"
2. Don Williams
3. Willie Nelson
4. "Hold Me"
5. number 7
6. RCA
7. S. Buckingham
8. W. Kemp
9. "That's That"
10. number 13

PART D

1. "My Heart"
2. Stevie Wonder
3. number 17
4. L.A., Babyface
5. number 19
6. Columbia
7. "Any Love"
8. "My Heart"
9. "You're Not My Kind of Girl"
10. "The Way You Love Me"

9 Scanning Statistical Tables

1. 57,360,000
2. 58,911,000
3. 12,426,000
4. 13,896,000
5. 31,218,000
6. 34,128,000
7. 4,300,000
8. 9,477,000
9. 486,000
10. 8,546,000
11. 8,368,000
12. 11,270,000
13. 27,047,000
14. 8,713,000
15. 57,678,000
16. 12,242,000

10 Scanning Newspaper Articles

PART A

1. about 140
2. no
3. no
4. 1,000 to 1,200
5. ear tags

PART B

6. reward, frustrating
7. double every year
8. winter
9. log cabin
10. since 1965

11 Scanning Documents

PART A

1. Article 4
2. Article 16
3. Article 9
4. Article 14
5. Article 11
6. Article 5
7. Article 13
8. Article 13
9. Article 15
10. Article 7

PART B

11. Article 23
12. Article 26
13. Article 17
14. Article 24
15. Article 27
16. Article 23
17. Article 20
18. Article 26
19. Article 21
20. Article 18

12 Scanning Reference Materials

1. 2,500,000
2. Virginia
3. no
4. November 30, 1782
5. yes
6. 550.986 kilometers
7. English Channel and the Atlantic
8. coal and iron ore
9. west
10. nearly 5 million

Words per Minute: Skimming

Directions: Using the *Minutes and Seconds* column or the *Seconds* column, find the time closest to your actual skimming time for each selection. In the columns under the selection titles, find the words-per-minute rate which corresponds to each skimming time.

Minutes and Seconds	Alexander Dolgun's Story	To Sir, with Love	Alive	Roots	Reincarnation and 13 Pairs of Socks	Sharks	My Early Life	Hour of Gold, Hour of Lead	Centennial	Body Language	Seconds
2:00	1145	1245	1135	1120	1185	1030	1210	1000	970	1035	120
2:10	1335	1150	1050	1035	1095	950	1115	925	900	955	130
2:20	1240	1065	975	960	1015	880	1035	860	835	885	140
2:30	1160	995	910	895	950	820	970	800	780	830	150
2:40	1085	935	855	840	890	770	910	750	730	775	160
2:50	1020	880	805	790	835	725	855	710	685	730	170
3:00	965	830	760	745	790	684	805	670	650	690	180
3:10	915	785	720	705	750	650	765	635	615	655	190
3:20	870	745	685	670	710	615	725	600	585	620	200
3:30	825	710	650	640	675	585	690	575	555	590	210
3:40	790	680	620	610	645	560	660	545	530	565	220
3:50	755	650	595	585	620	535	630	525	505	540	230
4:00	725	625	570	560	595	515	605	500	485	520	240
4:10	695	600	545	540	570	495	580	480	465	495	250
4:20	670	575	525	515	545	475	560	465	450	480	260
4:30	645	555	505	500	525	455	540	455	430	460	270
4:40	620	535	490	480	510	440	520	430	415	445	280
4:50	600	515	470	465	490	425	500	415	400	430	290
5:00	580	500	455	450	475	410	485	400	390	415	300
5:10	560	480	440	435	460	400	470	390	375	400	310
5:20	545	465	425	420	445	385	455	375	365	390	320
5:30	525	455	415	405	430	375	440	365	355	375	330
5:40	510	440	400	395	420	360	425	355	345	365	340
5:50	495	425	390	385	405	350	415	345	335	355	350
6:00	480	415	380	375	395	340	405	335	325	345	360
6:20	455	395	360	355	375	325	380	315	305	325	380
6:40	435	375	340	335	355	310	365	300	290	310	400
7:00	415	355	325	320	340	295	345	285	280	295	420
7:20	395	340	310	305	325	280	330	275	265	280	440
7:40	375	325	295	290	310	270	215	260	255	270	460
8:00	360	310	285	280	295	255	300	250	245	260	480
8:20	345	300	275	270	285	245	290	240	235	250	500
8:40	335	285	265	260	275	235	280	230	225	240	520
9:00	320	275	255	250	265	230	270	225	215	230	540
9:20	310	265	245	240	255	220	260	215	210	220	560
9:40	300	260	235	230	245	215	250	205	200	215	580
10:00	290	250	225	225	235	205	240	200	195	205	600

Progress Graph: Skimming

Directions: Write your comprehension score in the box under each selection title. Then put an *x* along the line under each box and title to show your words-per-minute rate for that selection.

	Alexander Dolgun's Story	To Sir, with Love	Alive	Roots	Reincarnation and 13 Pairs of Socks	Sharks	My Early Life	Hour of Gold, Hour of Lead	Centennial	Body Language

Comprehension Scores (left and right axes):

1000, 975, 950, 925, 900, 875, 850, 825, 800, 775, 750, 725, 700, 675, 650, 625, 600, 575, 550, 525, 500, 475, 450, 425, 400, 375, 350, 325, 300, 275, 250

Picture Credits

1 Alexander Dolgun's Story: An American in the Gulag: AP/Wide World Photos

2 To Sir, with Love: Photo courtesy of Columbia Pictures, Inc.

3 Alive: The Story of the Andes Survivors: J. P. Laffont/Sygma

4 Roots: © 1988 Copyright Capital Cities/ABC, Inc.

5 Reincarnation and 13 Pairs of Socks: Photo by Gary Bublitz/Bublitz Photography

6 Sharks: The Silent Savages: Jack Stein Grove/ Photo Edit

7 My Early Life: The Bettmann Archive

8 Hour of Gold, Hour of Lead: The Bettmann Archive

9 Centennial: Illustration from *Centennial* by James A. Michener, copyright © 1974. Reprinted by permission of Random House, Inc.

10 Body Language: Cover illustration from *Body Language* by Julius Fast, copyright © 1970, by Pocket Books

Scanning: All photos by Thomas Malloy